A Lo[illegible]
Boyhood

by Alan Neatby-Smith

ISBN 1-84173-019-X

1999

The Derbyshire Heritage Series

Happy Walking International Ltd.,
Unit 1, Molyneux Business Park,
Whitworth Road, Darley Dale,
Matlock, Derbyshire.
England.
DE4 2HJ

Happy Walking International Ltd.,
Unit 1,
Molyneux Business Park,
Whitworth Road,
Darley Dale,
Matlock,
Derbyshire
DE4 2HJ
Tel/Fax 01629 - 735911
E-Mail - john.merrill@virgin.net

Printed, bound, marketed and distributed by Happy Walking International Ltd.

First Published - August 1999.

ISBN 1-84173-019-X

British Library Cataloguing-in-Publication Data. A catalogue record of this book is available from the British Library.

Typeset and designed in Garamond - bold, italic, and plain 10pt. 12pt, 14pt and 18pt. by Max Hodnett.

Cover design © Happy Walking International Ltd. 1999. Front cover photo - One of several floods. Back cover - Alan Neatby Smith, his brothers and parents.

CONTENTS

FOREWORD

AS FAR back as I can remember I have been keen on nicknames, and had felt the lack of one, not even having acquired such a murky one as "Smudger"! In my schooldays, I even tried inventing one or two, but they never caught on.

I had to wait until my 24th year before I got my first proper one. For anyone similarly afflicted I will explain the process. On the mess-deck of our troopship taking us RAF chaps to South Africa, seated among a dozen completely unknown blokes, a broad Cockney opposite me enquired, "Wot do they call yer at 'ome?" Unprepared for such a personal confrontation I replied, "I'll give you three guesses." Quickly came back the first guess, "Tom". I opened my eyes wide and replied, "However did you guess?" and for 3¼ years I revelled in my new name.

On return to this country in 1944, my new sergeant, wishing to know his flock, enquired my first name. I naturally gave him three guesses. The first to come was "Bob". Once again I opened my eyes wide and asked him if he was clairvoyant, and rejoiced in my new-found name for the rest of my RAF career. Oh! with one exception: for a brief time, on a diesel course, the corporal-instructor was pleased to call me "Colonel".

This sort of pattern followed when, having met my future wife — then in the WAAF— and being of a timorous nature, feeling that my courtship by letter needed pepping up, I used to subscribe myself as "Oscar (the bold & bad!)". After our marriage, her family always knew me as "Oscar"

What Anthony Clare, the psychiatrist, would have made of all this I've no idea, but any reader in Long Eaton who feels any point in reading beyond this will find it quite easy to following the ramblings of plain Alan Smith.

PREFACE

I MIGHT as well come clean: there must be hundreds of chaps better qualified than I, by association and literary attainment, to chronicle such an epoch-making event as the early odyssey of a Long Eaton schoolboy.

For in a sense, although born in L.E. (as distinct from L.A.!), I was removed to Risley while still in nappies, in 1917, and did not return to the local metropolis until 1931. This translation from the impressive Queen Anne mini-mansion, known as the Latin House, to my new home in the cul-de-sac of Shakespeare Street (No. 55) must have been a pivotal event in my boyhood.

Although the rateable value of No. 55, S.S., L.E., may have been reduced by the much later erection of the urinal at the corner of College Street, the undoubted utility showed up the deficiencies of the Latin House, whose sanitary arrangements had not very materially altered since Queen Anne, 1706!

So I would ask any reader who may have got as far as this to bear with me for a brief history of the 14-year pre-L.E. life. After all, what is a three-mile gap these days, although then it was a cycle ride or Shanks's pony!

CHAPTER ONE
Risley — generally

IF THEY are right who claim that the first seven years of your life are most formative, I expect that if I were opened up they would find "Risley" written on my heart, rather than "Long Eaton", but I would like to think that my heart was big enough for the inscription of both!

Now Risley (Derbys) is a very different kettle of fish from Risley (Cheshire), the only thing in common being remand premises: huge in the latter case, tiny in the former, then occupying the outbuildings of the Elizabethan Risley Hall.

I was too young at the time to dig into the history of Risley Hall. The only former occupier (I believe) of whom I had heard was Sir Hugh Willoughby, the Elizabethan navigator, who perished with his crew when on a trading expedition to China. In my day, the celebrated occupier was Ernest Terah Hooley ("E.T." whispered by the villagers) whom some of the really elderly will remember as celebrated for being a millionaire twice and bankrupted twice and, I believe, gaoled once.

He must have been one of the original financial whizz kids who, as a company promoter, formed some of the best-known public companies, including Dunlop and Bovril. His confederate in these enterprises was the Long Eaton solicitor George (?) Wallis, who may also have done a stretch inside.

My only recollection of "E.T." was his occasional stately foray through the village, perched high in an old Rolls-Royce, and wearing his distinctive grey topper and, more often, accompanying some house guests on a rook-shooting expedition under the trees which lined the road and almost obscured the view of the Hall itself.

The only other celebrated person in the village was the poetess Teresa Hooley, whose precise relationship with "E.T." I never really knew, not moving in such exalted circles. I was privileged to meet her only twice: the first time at what may have been a garden party to which my parents and young brood must have been invited; the second, when I made a nostalgic visit to the old haunts from remotest Cornwall and tracked her down to a residential or nursing home in the Stanton area.

Of course, she didn't know me from Adam (nor I her!), but the completely unexpected visit out of the blue must have stirred some long-dormant memories, for I was enormously surprised, and pleased, when shortly after I was sent by an old friend a cutting from the *Long Eaton Advertiser* the following extract from what was Miss Hooley's regular column:

> "The other letter is from an old friend whom I have not seen since he was a small boy living with his parents at the Latin House, Risley. He now lives near Land's End, and his name is Alan Smith, or to give his full cognomen, C.A. Neatby Smith, Public Accountant. He is the son of the late Frederick Smith, L.D.S., who for many years practised as a dental surgeon in Long Eaton. My son and I were among his patients.
>
> "Mr and Mrs F. Smith had four sons, who are now "scattered to the four winds". Paul is at Southampton, Michael is at Cheltenham and Hugh is in Belfast. Alan found me after reading my letter in the *Sunday Times*. It is so nice to hear from him. He nostalgically remembers the peacocks at Risley Hall. So do I, and the way they used to eat the strawberries."

While on the subject of Miss Hooley, I was delighted to find, while browsing in a second-hand bookshop, a slim volume of her poems entitled "Gloom & Gleam". My only other recollection of her is her gift to us four boys (for our little "museum") of a small piece of Egyptian pottery, of a beautiful starling-egg blue, doubtless acquired in her married state (as Mrs. Butler) in Egypt.

It was not my intention of getting a local celebrity to introduce me to any readers, but as she has done so I must once again come clean. My "full cognomen" is a bit ersatz, and needs a bit of explanation. All my L.E. sojourn I was plain Alan Smith (not to be confused with more illustrious holders of the name, like the former Arsenal striker and the M.C.C. official). When I started to practise in remotest Cornwall, finding that there were two chartered accountants called Smith practising within the area, I adopted my wife's maiden name, Neatby (without hyphenation!). I therefore appeared in the telephone directory as Smith, C.A. Neatby, and it is not surprising that often clients told me that they "couldn't find me" in the directory.

All this ambiguity about my moniker came to a head recently when I got a letter from a confused head office of the National Insurance, asking exactly what my name was. I wrote back at some length, confessing the sordid details of my "cognomen", and was informed that hyphenating the Neatby and Smith was probably the best option. Since this did not involve any payment by way of deed poll, I agreed.

Since Teresa Hooley has introduced my father briefly, I will elaborate, also briefly. Our branch of the Smith tribe originated in the Boston, Lincs., area. There must be something in the air there conducive to the practise of dental surgery, for several related Smiths were thus engaged, and the most celebrated, Arthur Hopewell Smith, became a professor at Philadelphia University. My grandfather, Frederick, moved to Chesterfield, where he set up a successful practice in Burlington Street, which was later inherited by my late Uncle Harold, three years my father's senior.

My father had been deputed to start the first qualified dental practice in L.E., which was experiencing a lace boom, and because the two brothers felt they would never be able to run both practices in partnership, Harold retained the affluent established Chesterfield practice and "young" Fred the far newer L.E. one. Some small "cash adjustment" never really equated matters, and the L.E. branch has since been the more impoverished side of this particular Smith family.

As Teresa's column did not have room for my mother, I must do the needful. Margaret Rebecca Oldham Mason was the elder daughter by ten years of Margaret Elizabeth Mason, who had been a Nottinghamshire Oldham (Retford area, I believe) before marrying a Mr Mason, whose family had a tobacco factory at Chesterfield.

I know little about my mother's maiden life. At school at Chesterfield, she was a member of a female "triumvirate" *(I never knew the Latin for the female version!)*, which included Eva MacIntosh, who became the wife of Isaac Foot, of Pencrebar, Callington, Cornwall, the Plymouth lawyer and founder of the famous Liberal Foot family, of whom Michael Foot must be the best-known.

Trading on this flimsy relationship on one of my three annual solo cycle rides, I called at Pencrebar. Probably fortunately, the whole family was not at home, but I was shown round the estate by the caretaker, given a Cornish cream tea by his wife and despatched on my solitary way on brother Paul's Sun Wasp three-speed bike. This must seem pretty primitive to cyclists nowadays, only content with about 24 gears, and yet I recall one bloke pontificating about the merits of a single fixed gear!

The only other facet of her younger life I recall is that she had sworn that if she married and had children, they would be able to swim by the time they were two. Such are the vicissitudes of life that I was 14 when, with my three brothers, we were dragged to Radford Baths, Nottingham, to learn the mysteries of the breast-stroke! After seeing the film of Johnny Weismuller outstripping crocodiles with his wonderful crawl stoke, I inwardly cursed that swimming instructor for not having initiated us into this instead of the frog-like breast-stroke,

But as I would not be writing this now if my mother had not nursed me through a vicious double pneumonia and septicaemia before the advent of sulpha drugs and antibiotics, I must pay tribute to the indomitable character of a well-tried woman. As a result of this illness and a later one, both involving some four months' convalescence at home, she and I were in constant contact, and she would often unburden herself to me. Much did I learn, not only at Mother's knee, but at her mature stature.

I cannot omit a brief word about my primary school, Risley Lower Grammar. It was under the headship of "Gaffer" Finch, a short, stocky authoritarian, assisted by a mistress named Miss Topping (whom my dentist Uncle Harold insisted on referring to as Miss Stopping).

It seems inevitable that when she stood on a form to adjust a window fastening the boys nearest would find occasion to bend down, ostensibly to look for dropped pencils or whatever.

All I can remember of Gaffer's teaching was his emphasis on "parsing", and it may have been my modest ability to tell the difference between a noun and a verb which enabled me to achieve a cane-free existence for the duration of my stay. I was fortunate because, whether he did it for exercise or discipline, he was a dab hand with a lethal-looking cane.

The worst episode I can remember (I ought to give a warning notice: THIS NARRATION MAY CAUSE OFFENCE) involved Tom Shepherd, a spindly, sickly-looking lad who had a caliper on one leg. I'm not sure what sparked things off, but probably Tom had come up for his "three on each hand", and grabbed the cane on the first stroke. A wrestling match ensued, which naturally Gaffer won, and having recovered full use of the cane, lambasted poor Tom any and everywhere. Even the caliper clanged under the vicious blows.

Thinking back to that incident, I'm surprised that there was not a riot in the class, because one of the bigger boys — Ronald Duriez — had inherited the fighting gene from his burly French-born father, living in The Crescent of ten cottages in Breaston Lane. Gaffer Finch, not having graduated at the Sorbonne, was pleased to enquire at roll call: "Derezz?"

Fortunately, because of my placid nature, I never fell foul of Ronald, and quite liked his less violent younger brother, Charles. Whether it was my placidity or pudgy overgrown size, I never had a fight at either school, but at Risley I was intimidated by a little squirt. Perhaps I should have had some of Gaffer's guts.

Distasteful as the Tom Shepherd incident may sound to modern ears (and, I have to admit, to me at the time), I do not recall that he suffered any long-term ill effects and I now feel that the world would be a better place if teachers were allowed to exercise whatever punishment is necessary to maintain discipline.

Could this have been the same man who wrote in my autograph book these immortal lines:

To ALAN SMITH, that happy boy

Whose smiles so sweet and full of joy,

These lines in your new book I write,

And spoil the page which once was white.

Or was he hoping to get some discount on dental treatment from Father?

A chance modern reader of these lines could be forgiven for thinking they referred to Dickensian times (if they ever got around to reading Dickens).

Certainly, life was far simpler — a visit to the "picture palaces" to see a black-and-white film once or twice a year was a real treat. And for me the treat of treats was a very infrequent visit, *en famille*, to distant Nottingham — all of eight miles way — where, on passing the Kardomah Cafe, the smell of coffee made me feel like one of the Bisto Kids — walking on air. And very, very occasionally we actually went inside.

CHAPTER TWO
Up the Brook

LOOKING back on my young life in Risley, I suppose it could be divided into three main compartments — Up the Brook, Village Cricket and The Wilderness.

"Up the brook" consisted of frequently apparently aimless wanderings by a few of us village lads following the course of the brook with which the garden of the Latin House was blessed before it disappeared under the main road into I know not where. After a few hundred yards upstream, it flowed through fairly highish sloping banks of a pretty slippery clay and we precariously navigated these slopes, clinging to tree roots, branches or whatever was available, until we got to Dead Man's Pool in a sharpish bend of the brook.

Local boyish legend had it that it ws "seven times as deep as a man" and as it was too murky to see the bottom (probably 18 inches down) we gave it a wide berth. We never seemed to progress further than the spot where it placidly flowed through the bottom of Long Meadow, at the top of which was Patching's Farm. The term "Long" seemed to me a gross understatement for to my boyish eyes it seemed almost interminable.

Periodically, we would sit and rest on a convenient bit of bank. I cannot for the life of me recall the general topics of our pre or early teens: I don't recall "girls" featuring; there was little, if any, smoking — maybe the odd packet of five Woodbines. I think the idea was to compete in producing the most outrageous jokes about the inevitable "There was an Englishman, an Irishman and a Scotsman . . ." I don't often recall maligning Welshmen! I remember one corny offering on other lines ending, "Cow killed by cork in Kent", but fortunately I forget what preceded it. The final line may have caused my later penchant for alliteration.

Oh, yes! Before I leave "up the brook", in the last part of craggy banks, before Long Meadow, there was a neat uniform gash in the bank from the centre of the back from which issued a fine jet of spring water. There are no prizes for guessing a girl's name associated with this natural formation!

Mention of a girl's name reminds me that, at the age of ten, I developed a pronounced interest in one of the village girls, whose family lived near the "four lane ends" and whose father worked in Hayward's nursery, and she duly came to Risley Lower Grammar School. Stella Jacklin was 12 and had the lustrous eyes and colouring of a Spanish or Italian girl. Everybody seemed to know of my interest and were always encouraging me to kiss her, which I never did. Years later, I learned that my eldest brother, Paul, was also smitten.

Probably before the village lads episodes, I remember the odd family jaunts up Chappell's fields to the farm track (which passed Teresa Hooley's entrance) up to Top Farm in the far, far distance. Having survived this long climb my aching legs would gradually recover as we plodded over reasonably level ground to the Blasted Oak.

This was not a pub, but a favourite landmark, and we seldom progressed beyond this pathetic tree. It was on the road leading down from this that I later tracked down Teresa Hooley's retirement home. Needless to say, the Blasted Oak featured in my nostalgic visits from Cornwall.

Father sometimes accompanied us on these walks, Mother never; the poor soul could not have had enough energy for this after managing four thoughtless lads and trying to cope with the running of the large Latin House single-handed. Now and then she would have some help from one of the village girls, apparently chosen for her unbecoming looks — for obvious reasons.

As Father never had a car he naturally did a lot of cycling and so, indulging himself, acquired a specially large comfortable saddle. I also had the pleasure of this indulgence when, on one of my rare visits I stayed with my old friend Les Statham in Breaston and found that he had somehow acquired Father's old saddle. Truly home from home!

I suppose Father must have cycled the three miles from Risley to his surgery in L.E., but there came a time when he started catching the Trent bus — immediately outside the Latin House — and changing at Sandiacre on to a Barton bus for L.E. I remember one embarrassing moment when the Trent bus automatically stopped at the Latin House to collect Pa. He didn't turn up and the driver asked me if I would chase him up.

I whipped back into the house and eventually had to go back and tell the driver that I couldn't find him. I don't suppose it mattered in those palmy days if the bus timetable suffered the odd ten-minute or so setback.

I can't say I blamed Mother, having to grapple with the rearing of four growing lads (Father having semi-opted out), for sending us to bed by 8.30 pm. So it was that, in summer, having been so despatched, I used to kneel at my bedroom window, fixing my eyes on Chappell's field (sometimes called "the park"), beyond the graveyard, watching cricket still being played or practised. The crack of leather on willow was music to my ears and doubtless contributed to the ensuing sleep.

Mention has already been made of the antiquated sanitary arrangements of the Latin House, and Chappell's field has just reminded me of them. This was the spare-time (?) duty, after dark, of one of Mr Chappell's farm workers named Alf Last.

About five feet high and built like a gorilla, he would come and heft the night-soil buckets on to his shoulders, sway to the night-soil cart patiently pulled by a cart-horse, for eventual discharge on to some other of Mr Chappell's fields. I never heard that he tripped up during this odorous operation.

Because of the nightly timing of the operation, dear old Alf was a semi-mythical character, but on Sunday evenings he would appear cleaned and polished for Evensong, grinning away under the watchful eye of his churchwarden-boss, Mr H B Chappell. I wonder what dear old H B would have said about all this artificial fertilizer racket?

He became a valued friend of my parents and eventually had the unpleasant task of despatching the aged and badly neglected donkey, Horace, to whom he had become quite attached, and to whom you will be introduced shortly. H B had an engaging habit of filing his horny nails on a sandstone cap of the wall outside the Latin House. The grooves this made could perhaps in the fulness of time be construed as Runic signs of some old Risley love affair.

CHAPTER THREE
Village Cricket

CRICKET — village variety — was my main interest, and the venue for this was Chappell's Field, which was an ordinary grazing field of rough pasture, with a pronounced slope, out of which had been levelled a mown square, which was fenced off.

The fence kept the cows off the pitch, but did not prevent them doing their business outside, and many runs were made while the unfortunate fielder was extricating the ball from a cowpat and wiping it on adjacent long grass before his return throw. Needless to say, the outfield could not have been called fast, and if you wanted a boundary it was best to go for a six.

I was reluctantly prevailed upon to captain the boys' team, but would do so only as joint captain with Percy Eyre, Jnr., my senior by a year or so who later, in the men's team, produced such prodigious off-breaks that even Shane Warne would have applauded. Although I must have shown some batting promise — there were some suggestions that I ought to go to "Derby nets" for professional testing and tuition — I never had the killer instinct and my maximum score at my boyish best was 37.

Then followed the ludicrous episode when I was elevated to the senior team and, horror of horrors, asked to open the batting. This imposed such an overwhelming sense of responsibility that I lost all my scoring strokes and became a dedicated stone-waller, the object being to keep one end intact and let the other end do the scoring (if any). My tenacity sometimes resulted in my "carrying my bat" with a mere ten or so runs to my credit (most onlookers would have preferred "to my debit").

In fact, a few years later, playing on West Park, a spectator was heard to say in exasperation: "He's got shoulders (I was 6 feet and 13 stones), why doesn't he use them?" Fair comment — in fact, all too fair.

In my earliest days, there was a tendency to have to choose between George Heath and Percy Walter George Eyre as the local hero. Mr Heath, a farmer who had a trademark stance when his front foot rested on the heel, as though he hoped to trap a well-pitched ball by slapping down the toe, must have retired fairly soon, leaving Percy ("Uncle Perce" to us youngsters) in complete charge.

He had played for Derbyshire in his youth (I'm not sure whether 1st or 2nd XI) and certainly knew his stuff, both batting and bowling. I remember him once scoring 98, which was no mean feat, the outfield being as it was, but I don't remember how many came from "cowpat" runs. He was also a wily, left-arm spin bowler.

He was also naturally senior coach, but the only advice I can remember was: "Front foot towards the pitch of the ball, Alan." I suppose he must have had some slogan for back-play. The "Uncle Perce" must have arisen from the presence of his two nephews, Percy and Lewis. The former was my joint captain of the boys' team and the latter my junior by a couple of years. Percy, slow, right-arm vicious off-breaks; Lewis, slow, left-arm, and neither had Uncle Perce's batting genes. Both were well over six feet and later came successfully through the war in the Guards.

Uncle Perce was the village postmaster and with his wife, Aunt Else, kept the village shop which nestled behind the Latin House. It was approached over a bridge that straddled my favourite brook just before it disappeared in the Latin House garden. It was there that we spent our Saturday pennies (the ones that didn't go into little money boxes, or that we had prised out of them).

Many years later, on a rare visit, I called to see them. They hadn't a clue who I was so I gracefully demonstrated the "front foot to the pitch of the ball" technique, but was rewarded with a baffled look. I suppose I should have realised, because he must have been 84, and I believe it was shortly after this that he was mugged at the shop and died not very long afterwards.

Also in the team were brother Mick, Jim Stroud (of the Strodex Corset Co., L.E.), Len Savidge (of Bouyant Upholstery), Sid Joynes, a printer (I believe with Hassall & Lucking, L.E.), Bill Fisher, son of the scorer, and the Sumter brothers, Hedley and Leslie. The latter was an erratic fast bowler. I forget Hedley's speciality, but I remember him for his narration of an anecdote about an incident in a hockey match he was playing with my Latin master, John Crompton, which shall be narrated hereafter.

CHAPTER FOUR
The Wilderness

I HAVE never known how the name originated. The wilderness proper was the bottom area of an inverted L-shaped piece of land which Father rented from the landlords of the Latin House, the Ecclesiastical Commissioners. This bottom part skirted the brook after a couple of huge willow trees, which strangely enough were still producing leaf although their trunks were almost completely hollow.

There was a rough gate with a rudimentary lock — this was a bit superfluous because it was dead easy to climb over a poor fence. However, once through the gate (or over the fence) one met some splendid beech, horse chestnut and hornbeam trees, intermingled with assorted undergrowth and little windy paths. I had a perfectly formed "throne" high up in the best beech tree.

There were also various old apple trees, including a huge russet, and a special one with pale-green fruit, almost the same size (and as sweet) as a cherry tomato. It was probably a crab apple with some sweet genes implanted by a thoughtful bird. There was a gorgeous overgrown wildness about the place, which probably accounted for the name.

Then through a home-made gate in the fence, you found yourself in an orchard with splendid damson trees and, in the top left-hand corner, The Hut, which Father had converted from a goat shed into a weekend holiday hut. It soon needed an extension as the family grew. Then the top of the inverted L provided another orchard with more apple and pear trees and, boy, did I gorge myself! I must have kept a whole host of doctors away.

I must not forget to introduce you to an early entrant. This was the donkey, Horace, bought ostensibly to enable us to learn to ride. Horace had other ideas, and none of us four boys ever mastered him. But he became a great favourite with visiting friends and he took a great liking to Mother. He was always around during our weekend picnics, and always gravitated towards Mother. At times, it looked almost as though he was trying to sit on her knee as she reclined in a deckchair, and he was most reluctant to be moved.

In addition to this inverted L-shaped land there was another adjacent orchard (which we later had to give up), in which there was space among yet more pear and apple trees for a tennis court, to which poor Mother contributed most of the hard work. We also had a small cricket pitch for family knockabouts. I have to confess that at this stage I went through a "mardy" adolescent phase when I shared with my Victorian hero, Dr W. G. Grace, a great reluctance to be adjudged out. But I like to believe that this was confined to the family performances and that in the outer world I was more prepared to "walk" than the odd Australian Test batsman.

Dear old Pa had the most round-arm action I have ever seen, a cross between underarm and overarm.

Another indispensable part of my Risley sojourn must now be introduced. I don't recall exactly how it came about, but during the black days around the year of the General Strike (1926), and possibly earlier, Father and Mother had gone out of their way to "look after" a Breaston family going through hard times. Herbert Allen, being out of work, was made part-time handyman at the wilderness and I learned later that Father used to take round on his bike a full Christmas dinner to a most grateful Mrs Allen, then with two young boys.

Brother Hugh tells me that Herb. also became part-time handyman at 55, Shakespeare Street, which must have been very much appreciated by my mother. He became a great favourite with us boys; eventually the tide turned and he got a job at British Celanese at Spondon, where his steadiness enabled him to look after three machines. Dear old Herb. never lost his gratitude to my parents for their quiet help.

I think it almost broke Mother's heart when we left the Latin House for L.E. in 1930; apart from the fondness for the house itself (however hard it must have been for her to run it) I suspect she must have missed the wilderness terribly. On my subsequent rare visits to L.E. I never failed to pay a nostalgic visit to the wilderness. Alas, much has been altered — The Hut has disappeared, also all the apple and damson trees and most of the pear trees.

The wooded part has altered least, but the weeds and brambles were more than waist-high and had to be forced through. I recognised my old beech throne, but declined to enthrone myself.

It's strange how you can become attached to things. Although we were at the Latin House for only 14 years, it had so entered into me that, long after, when I heard that a following family of Williams had been there 30-odd years, I felt they were interlopers!

The last two years of my sojourn there introduced me to to Long Eaton proper, for having won two minor scholarships at Risley Lower Grammar School, I started with my brothers the three-mile cycle ride to the secondary on Tamworth Road. This first bit was fairly hair-raising.

After cycling up to the "four lane ends", we turned right to go down Bostock Lane (Bricky Lane to us), which was a steep descent at right-angles to the no longer existing canal. But at the time it definitely did exist and if our brakes had failed or we had misjudged the exceedingly sharp right-hand turn on to the towpath, we would have ended in the drink.

Long after, during a nostalgic visit, I was dismayed to find that the old "cut" had disappeared as a result of all the reconstruction necessary because of the new M1. Possibly on this same visit I was taken by Les Statham, with whom I was staying, on to the bridge over the M1 by Pegg's Farm.

After some years never having moved out of a small area of really rural Cornwall, I was utterly flabbergasted and disorientated, thinking that the M1 was going east-west instead of south-north.

CHAPTER FIVE
School antics

HAVING successfully crossed the canal, after Longmoor Lane, Curzon or Breedon Street, Derby Road, The Green and Market Place, we found ourselves in Tamworth Road, at the secondary school. I suppose it must have been a bit of an eye-opener for us, never having had sisters, suddenly to be plunged into a co-ed school, but I must confess that don't recall much about the first two or three forms.

For this reason I have availed myself of the kindness of Miss Eileen Adams, of Beeston, who has very kindly lent me her copy of the Jubilee 1960 book of Long Eaton Grammar School. The information dispensed thereform will be of far more interest to readers than my sparse and feeble recollections.

The school had been under the headship, from the very earliest days, of Mr Samuel Clegg. He must have been quite a remarkable man, for I read that "he had an enthusiasm for literature, art and knowledge in general which could not have been bettered by any formal academic qualification; he had an eye for promising young men, a quality well illustrated by his appointment of C B Fawcett and F L Attenborough and he had 'the gift of leading and controlling amicably a team of much higher academic qualifications'. He was also a tried administrator who had an unequalled knowledge of the school."

I also learn that "in this year (1913) two old scholars joined the staff: Mr F L Attenborough, who was to stay for two years before going to Cambridge and who, after marrying Mary Clegg, Mr Clegg's daughter, was to become Principal of Leicester University College and be, perhaps, more widely known as the father of Richard and David Attenborough . . ."

Had he any inkling, I wonder, that the former would be ennobled for his vast contribution to the film and theatre world (doubtless sparked by Mr Clegg's early encouragement of literature and art and associated subjects), and that the latter would become a household name in bringing us the wonders of the natural world? Not only did he encourage art, but he wrote about it — "Drawing and Design, a four-year course in art teaching for secondary schools". The Jubilee book tells us that "everything in the book has been proved in school".

So I am somewhat reluctant to report that even he was not infallible, for I am told that after my initial interview with him, my parents were informed that I would be a judge — apparently because I thought of both sides before answering questions. Or had he really guessed that my apparent care in answering was due to my not having a clue how to answer?

I did not know at the time that Mr Mansfield was senior master, having arrived from Manchester in 1914. Always known as "Tashy", although I remember him only as clean-shaven, he was a small man, but always completely in charge. Although at times he could be a bit severe and sarcastic, he was mainly genial. My main recollection of him is during French lessons, when a pupil hesitating over translation came out with ". . . er", which would be met by Tashy's deadpan "eggs". He must have been a remarkably useful all-rounder, staff-wise, as he had a very practical bent, including among other things photography and stage lighting.

The closest I got to him was in the sixth form when I evinced an interest in German — then not in the curriculum — and he went out of his way to give me a weekly evening lesson at his home, using one of Mother's school text books. My last memory of him, as a then very elderly man, was in a Breaston pub, on one of my visits from Cornwall. On introducing myself he was pleased to declaim: "By Tre, Pol and Pen, ye shall know the Cornishmen." I must have lost my Derbyshire accent by then.

John Crompton must, I suppose, have been my favourite teacher and I sometimes wondered whether the fact that he had learned that I was living at the Latin House, Risley, made any bond between us. I recall cutting out an advert. by the Crompton Electric Bulb Co., showing an electric bulb surmounted by a scholar's mortar-board, and left it on his desk with an unsigned "To a favourite master".

I never remember him other than half-bent, seldom leaving his desk, and it was a terrific surprise to learn in 1999 that he had continued teaching (and become senior master) until 1960. I was given an insight into his earlier life when Hedley Sumter, of the Risley cricket team, knowing that I had gone to the Secondary, recounted how he had played hockey with John Crompton, who had been a dashing player.

He recalled how in one match John must have been knocked (or fallen) down, and as he lay prone for some time, Hedley asked him if he was all right. The reply came: "I'm all right, Hedley, I'm having a pee."

One of my least favourite memories is of Mr Aucken, the chemistry master, waxing wrathful and throwing chalk at pupils, and it was probably this which made me opt for Latin when in Form 3 we had to choose between this and chemistry. With hindsight, I wish I could have pursued both. I suppose my choosing Latin made me feel that I was on the arts side instead of science, and I certainly don't recall much of Mr Bowman Beer's physics classes. Whether through diffidence or lack of interest, my elbows were never sharp enough to let me get anywhere near some practical demonstration. This applied to later demonstrations in the RAF.

Mr Bowman Beer was one of the original staff when I started, but a year after arrived Mr R J Pritchard (I never heard his first name), science, of whom I remember least of all. He was tallish, quiet, with a small, buttoned-up mouth, and found difficulty in pronouncing his "Rs". Two years after, in 1931, came three others: Mr Macdonald, maths, as a replacement for Mr Fletcher, who was to become Dr Fletcher, of Liverpool University, and Mr Joe W Parsons, English and commercial subjects.

While Mr Bowman Beer was tall and gangly, the others were small: Macdonald quite slender, but very agile, always dashing about, pulling faces and gesticulating, and brother Hugh tells me that he also threw chalk, and more accurately than Aucken; Parsons, stockier, dark and Celtic-looking, with a very firm jaw.

The third was Raymond Parmenter, music and history, large and pudgy, whom I remember mainly for his drilling us in the rendition of Blake's "Jerusalem". How the WI would have lapped it up! He must have been a pretty strict marker in history, because while it was never a good subject of mine I remember once getting a mark of 40%, and being praised for it. How much lower must my previous efforts have been.

Any lady reader will doubtless be more interested in the female staff, led by Miss Lily Taylor, whose long sojourn, from 1905, was to last for 41 years. One of my treasured memories is of seeing dear old John sitting quietly in Lily's tiny office with his arm around her.

She remains for me a model of ultra-quiet authority. I recall the gracious way in which she felt she had to restrain my burgeoning manhood which drove me to see how many of the wooden wall panels could withstand my sledgehammer fist without cracking. How exquisitely different from Gaffer Finch's technique. Of course, you never really know. Had it not been for her quiet ministry I might have ended up slogging it out in some obscure boxing ring, or working as a "panel-basher" for some clapped-out, back-street, banger repairer.

Miss Jessie Drake, history, whose seniority dated from 1911, must have given me up before my brief burgeoning under Raymond Parmenter. Her no-nonsense approach was also that of her close friend, Miss Connie Silk, geography, who arrived in 1917. Her skirt was *just* short enough for me to admire her *gastrocnemii*, which must have served her well in her county tennis games. For athleticism, there could not have been much difference from Virginia Wade or Martina Navratilova; but I never knew whether she was left- or right-handed.

All I can remember from the geography lessons is my fascination with the position of Durban on the South African coast, and it is typical of my indisciplined self that I missed the opportunity of seeing it in the flesh, so to speak, during my 3¼ years' RAF service there. How was I to know that, though we would normally have been repatriated from Durban (on which I was relying), an outbreak of something or other would cause us to be shipped out from Capetown, where I had been all the time.

Miss Rigby (could she have been Winnie?) came on the scene about this time, as art and gym mistress, and also as a curvacious blonde. I seem to remember that her gym-slip was a bit short for a mixed school. But possessed of a fairly strong family streak for art, my interest was strictly professional, although I must confess to one remarkably unprofessional incident.

My eldest brother, Paul, then at Nottingham Art School, had supplemented that course by acquiring a very large format book which formed the course material for the Press Art School, a London correspondence school. I became fasçinated by the pictorial contents of this and, through sheer bonhomie, I lent it, without Paul's knowledge, to Miss Rigby. I never got it back.

Somewhere about the 1980s, one one of my visits from Cornwall, I plucked up courage, visited the school, confessed my misdemeanour to the secretary and was kindly invited to see if it was by any chance in the library and, of course, it wasn't.

If there is room on my heart for anything besides Risley and Long Eaton, I think I would settle for Press Art School.

It may have been this infusion of new blood in the staff which precipitated the formation of the "house" system, needless to say based on Mr Clegg's vision of 1912, when he wrote what was to become the school song, "Derby, Leicester, Notts are we . . .", hence the house names, Derwent, Trent and Soar. Initially, it was a sore point with me to find myself allocated to the last.

A pity the little River Erewash could not have been accommodated, since it did the job of separating Derbyshire from Nottinghamshire in our neck of the woods, fortunately leaving LE in the former

The prefect system also appears to have been instituted about this time (although I have to confess that I do not recall a single example), and also speech day, at which I do remember Mr Roberts intoning: "My lords, temporal and spiritual, ladies and gentlemen . . ." One of the lords temporal was the Earl of Crawford and Balcarres, who, on grasping my hand for the second time at prizegiving, said: "You've been here before!":

One of the times was for an award in calligraphy, the prize being a leather-bound three volumes of Shakespeare's works, but I can't for the life of me remember what the other one was for.

A scrutiny of the Roll of Honour boards would not have revealed the names of any Prime Ministers or other popular public figures, but of a few who had reached the top of the several vocations. I have just learned that they would not have been available for scrutiny, having been removed on the restructuring as a community school.

So once again I rely on the Jubilee book for the names of the following distinguished personages:

Academics

Professor H Godwin, FRS	Professor of Botany, Cambridge
Dr D Bagguley	Fellow of Brasenose College, Oxford
Mr R Alton	Fellow & Bursar of S. Edmund Hall, Oxford
Mr A B Clegg	Director of Education, West Riding
Miss Audrey Butler	Headmistress, Stourbridge Cty. High for Girls
Mr F L Attenborough	Formerly Principal, Univ. Coll., Leicester
Mr B Grimley	Lecturer, Liverpool University

Industrialists

Dr W L Patrick	Managing Director, Pilkingtons Ltd.
Mr K W Palmer	Managing Director, ICI Heavy Ind. Sect.
Dr S Slater Grimley	Research Manager, Canadian Industries Ltd.
Dr G I Hobday	Director, Boots Cash Chemists
Mr J W Leivers	" " " "

Other

Dr W E Gye, FRS	Formerly head of Cancer Research
Mr T C Sharman, OBE	A distinguished Foreign Office official

CHAPTER SIX

More school personalities

ALTHOUGH when starting school I must have been a gangling, oversized lad, the seniors always seemed immeasurably bigger and older, and only a little less awesome than the masters. I remember, particularly, flaxen-haired Tommy Sharman, son of a humble Castle Donington railway worker, a brilliant Latinist who, in 1930, won a State Scholarship and was reputed to be destined for high places.

I never heard that he had got any higher than consul at Riga, but I am probably wrong. About his time would have been tall, dark, Eton-cropped Brenda Clarke (also from Castle Donington?), who already seemed to be grown up, and Winnie Feber, whose physiognomy I don't recall at all, but whose cerebral attainments in the mathematical field, together with those of Brenda, were made known to us lesser plodders. They must have been mathematician Fletcher's pride and joy.

Any lady reader rejoicing in the name of Joan may be interested to read of:

JOAN KNOTT —	first woman in the country in the Civil Service Administrative Branch Examination
JOAN GODFREY —	first woman in the Assistant Tax Inspectors' Examination
JOAN HURLEY —	who won a State Scholarship in 1937.

Long before my time there was Keith Palmer, of a Sandiacre family, a brilliant dye-chemist, who became head of the ICI plant at Billingham, before being head-hunted for a still higher position in the USA. So even the humble LECSS was involved in the brain drain! One Saturday I watched Keith bowl at Sandiacre cricket ground. It must have been very dry for both he and the ball seemed to disappear in a cloud of dust, and he put me in mind of Harold Larwood.

His younger brother, Neville, my senior by four years, also ended up in the North of England, managing a power station, and also bowled, but at a much reduced pace, for Risley. About Neville's time there must have been Mary Cordingley, with a sublime English beauty and already sufficiently developed, to my young eyes, to provide a noble bosom on which a confused adolescent could rest his aching head.

Not far behind would have been the eldest of the Smedley trio, from the Beeston area I believe, who, with his younger siblings, were universally known as Gale, Breeze and Draught, the last being in my form and, I believe, Breeze in brother Mick's. Gale resides in my memory for his charming injunction when, as a server of Mrs Frost's school meals, he invariably said: "Get it, darn yer, that or nowt."

This brings me back to Neville's contemporaries. Brother Paul and his greatest friend, Les Statham, of Breaston, were later both in the art world, Paul having gone to Nottingham Art School and Les to Derby Art School. Paul became a commercial artist at the Carrington Studio in Nottingham, did photo-retouching on *Picture Post* at Watford and finally, having married a Southampton girl, ended up as a cartographer at the Ordnance Survey HQ at Southampton, where he died in 1981.

Les served his apprenticeship at the Offset Press on Nottingham Road and became a skilled chromo-litho artist, ending up at Rolls-Royce in charge of their graphic departments. Paul and Les must have had a very real affinity, one of their most pleasurable pastimes being trips in Paul's MG to quiet country pubs well out of the LE area. I have heard of occasions when, on entering some pubs (as two nearly six-footers) they were met with a frantic clearing of tables as some guilty consciences quickly reacted.

Now Alec Lawley comes to mind, and very soon lost track of, but I recently heard that his younger sister, Ruth, progressed to the other side of my fence — the Tax Inspectorate, at Nottingham, one inspector I have never had to cross swords with.

One of her contemporaries must have been Harold Horner, who for years seemed to be the secretary of the Old Scholars' Association. It may have been my imagination, but he always seemed to arouse more contemptuous mirth than respect, but he was certainly a sticker, and was quite irrepressible. I believe he ended up teaching at Draycott.

Jumping a couple of years, we come to brother Mick's form, two above mine, and we have a candidate for the Honours Board. Ivan Hobday, from Breaston, whom I remember as a gangly youth, eventually matured into Sir Gordon Hobday, chairman of the prestigious Boots Cash Chemists.

Johnny Whitaker, whose sliding tackle at football was my first introduction to this manoeuvre, became a sort of role model for me and after getting a fairly unexpected degree at "Notts Coll" regrettably paid the final price as an RAF pilot. Brother Mick — probably the most gifted of us four brothers — served his time as a cabinet-maker with the local firm of Bartlett and Worth, later working for the top Broadway firm Gordon Russel Ltd., and on outbreak of war worked on wooden aircraft, including the Mosquito.

Later, he moved from the work-bench to the drawing-board, and among other things was involved in the draughtsmanship for a part of the original Concorde. He had moved to Cheltenham and there produced my only nephew, Geoffrey, who became a chartered architect in the Telford area. Mick died in 1997, aged 82.

I don't recall much of the form below Mick's, except that it housed one of the best sporting all-rounders, George Breed, whose cannonball shot at goal, after a lightning twist, was particularly memorable. More of George in a later section on cricket.

One of his year was Ernie Plackett, from the Sandiacre haulage firm, whose sudden twist with the ball after a dash down the left wing I learned to time fairly accurately. His elder brother, "Charry" Plackett, was one of the star pupils of the Art Room, and only comes to mind from one unusual episode. For some reason a hair had been pulled from among his incipient chest hair and we were gathered round staring at a spot of real blood.

Dennis "Tagger" Taylor, the fastest runner in the school, of whom we shall hear more later, was around at this time. He and I came into collision in a house soccer match, in which I upended him in what I still consider was a fair shoulder-charge, but as he was the fastest runner in the school and I was only a gangling near-six-footer, the decision went against me. As my favourite master, John Crompton, backed up the decision I can't accuse him of favouritism.

Coming now to my form, the first mention must go to Katie ("Swot") Boyes, from York Avenue, Sandiacre, undisputed top of the form year by year: a quiet, blond, serene girl, ethereally fragile-looking, but obviously tough enough to achieve first-class honours in economics at Cambridge.

There was nothing fragile-looking about statuesque Betty ("Jigger") Lloyd, nor her ginger-haired cousin Joyce ("Jo") Tunnicliffe, both from Breaston; carroty-haired Muriel ("Mudge") Miles, of Wellington Street (of whom more later); Margaret Taylor, sister of Dennis, Hermione ?, the plainest girl, with steel specs and long plaits, but what a good sport she was.

I have to admit that my boyish admiration for the opposite sex resided not in my own form but in the one above. For in a brief sojourn in the sixth form, after matriculation, I encountered Margaret Dalgleish, of the mineral water firm, and then in second-year sixth. She was not a conventionally "pretty" girl and I was not put off by her nickname — Maggie Dagger — but admired her for being both the champion slow cyclist and one of the fastest 80-yarders.

I suppose I was also attracted by the fact that she seemed to be the only girl remotely interested in me. Being somewhat unnaturally diffident, I was reluctant to tackle the problem head-on and attempted to employ Mudge Miles as a go-between. Dear old Mudge never seemed to do her stuff and only a much later revelation made me understand that she would have preferred to have played first fiddle.

Immediately after I left, and commenced my articles at 34 Market Place, I took my afternoon cup of tea to the window, hoping to see Maggie cycling past on the way home to 180 Wollaton Road, Nottingham, and afterwards we managed a very decorous and short-lived courtship.

Having previously mentioned my placid nature, I would hate to think that I had given any reader the impression that I was more of a mouse than a man. It may have been shortly after I left the sixth form than I found that a small French exchange teacher was paying more attention to Maggie than I considered necessary. Having established the whereabouts of his lodgings, I went there one evening and as he stood in the doorway, I towered over him, and in stilted schoolboy English (unmixed with crude Anglo-Saxon) informed his that unless he desisted I might find it necessary to push his Gallic teeth past his epiglottis.

Looking back with horror, I recognise my foolishness. But for a Merciful Providence he might have had a flick-knife under his armpit or the French equivalent of a skean dhu inside his sock, and might even have come out top of his épée class!

And to think that within seven years or so we would be fighting (briefly) with, and not against, our gallant French allies.

Prime mention among the boys of my class must go to Charles Edward ("Wag") Owen, who, although quite a bit below my average eighth place in class, manifested signs of mathematical genius, and it was believed that he was destined for high office. For years I had laboured under the impression that this hope had been quashed by his death in a motor-cycle accident shortly after leaving school. However, by a pure fluke I saw the name Owen, CE, in the *Daily Telegraph* obituaries a few years ago and learned that he had died at Bournemouth, aged 62, after what must have been a successful career in the higher reaches of the IBM computer firm, and probably included invaluable backroom wartime work.

My ageing neurons do not allow me to recall many of my male form-mates, but I will do my best.

Doug ("Cudge") Harrison, of Wellington Street, a small bespectacled lad, the fastest 100-yarder in his year, seemed to have more attachment for me than I for him. I think he went on to a degree in chemistry at Notts College. Arthur ("Mary") Edwards, so-called after his elder sister; George ("Draught") Smedley, a mischievous imp, and the complete opposite of his big brother "Gale"; Ted Mercer, a quiet lad who went to Stanton Ironworks; Colin Burke, memorable only for three things — he could easily have been Shane Warne's youthful double, he was the only one I came near to having a fight with, and his persistent rendition during morning assembly of "Our Shield and Defender" as "our shield and tin fender".

Bobby ("Flabby") Turner went to Stanton Ironworks in the transport section, which experience would have served him well as a major during the war. He had the use, for practice, of the organ of Mount Tabor Methodist Chapel, but instead of hymns he played popular songs, of which I best remember "Red Sails in the Sunset".

Donald Grist always seemed to be smiling, a natural optimist; "Dutch" Hutchinson drew a beautiful indian-ink Schneider Trophy seaplane in my autograph book and later lost his life in an RAF land plane; Donald Kirk, of College Street, a quiet lad with thick, wavy auburn hair.

By now the house system had been instituted and if memory serves me correctly, Derwent was most often top house, I sometimes wonder how random was the allocation of pupils. I don't recall very much detail, but it must go on record that the prodigious all-rounder, George Breed, Derwent, knocked spots off us by throwing the cricket ball a magnificent 103 yards. However much I wound myself up, I never managed more than about 60.

Even George had something to learn from an Eton College boy who apparently knocked up 130 yards! I wonder how this compares with professional cricketers?

I can't even remember who captained Soar House at cricket, whether Ken Bettle, of College Street, or myself. But I do remember that he and I seemed to share the bowling, and often shared the wickets 50-50. I had always been regarded from Risley days as principally a batsman, but for Soar I developed a high shoulder action which enabled me to maintain a very straight ball and little short of a yorker. But once again I cannot remember having been called upon to bowl for the school team, having been relegated to opening batsman with George Breed. Masochistically, I always chose to take "first bowl".

Living only a few stone-throws from Trent College, it would have been strange if we did not come into some contact with the scholars, but there never seemed to be any about the town. Father was visiting dental surgeon to the college, but we learned nothing from him.

I remember one occasion when the public must have been admitted to a rugby match and I had my first glimpse of the celebrated Prince Obolensky, with his shock of golden hair pushed back by the wind as he flew down the wing. This was a preview of a later occasion when he did a like service for his country in an international game. Am I right in believing that soon afterwards he gave his life for his country in the ensuing war?

The headmaster at that time was G F Bell, and I remember writing to him after I had left school suggesting that a cricket match be arranged between an XI from our old scholars and one from his college. Alas, it fell on deaf ears — probably most fortunately for us since they would most likely have murdered us.

Risley, generally -

The Latin House, Risley.

Risley Lower Grammar School - 1925
Back row - 1. Percy Eyre 2. ? Dean 8. Brother Mick
Middle row - 1. H.J.Finch 2. Billy Rouse 4. Ada Bosworth 5. ? Moon 6. ? Griffen 7. Muriel Draper 8. Les Griffen.
Front row - 2. ? Green 8. Brother Hugh 10. Chas Duriez.

My family - Brothers - Hugh, Paul, Michael and myself with Mother and Father in front.

One of several floods. from left to right - Mr. Nichols (caretaker), Arthur Edwards, Donald Grist, Bobby Turner, myself, brother Mick.

Up the brook -

The Blasted Oak.

The bridge over the brook where brother Hugh tells us in Chapter 10, page 48, he was bitten by a ....dog.

Village Cricket

Risley Cricket Club, 1932.
Back row - H. Gough, ? Wells, Mick, ??, Les Sumter, Mr. Fisher, Joe Eyre.
Middle row - Mr. Temple, Sid Joynes, myself, Hedley Sumter, Len Savidge, Percy Eyre jnr, Percy Eyre Snr.
Front row - Lewis Eyre, Bill Fisher.

The School Team a few years after my departure.
Standing - J.W.Parsons, ??, Harry Makins, ??, Ray Parminter, Wally Tunnicliffe, J.B.Crompton. Kemp.
Sitting - Len Upton, Jack Astill, Reg Alton (Capt), Hugh, Paul Smith (no relation!).

Quiet picnic at the Wilderness. Horace with Father & Moter.

H.B. Chappell, of Golden Brook Farm, Cricket Landlord, natural fertilizer specialist, Churchwarden.

Weekend at the Wilderness. Family group with Herb at right.

Sixth Form get-together at Margaret Dalgliesh's home.
From left to right - Balmer, Donald Grist, Doug Harrison, Ken Bettle, Girvan Dalgliesh, Charles Owen, George Breed, Bingham, Joyce Tunnicliffe, Muriel Miles, Joan Knott, Katie Boyes, Joan Godfrey, Margaret Dalgliesh.

The School before 1914.

Mr. S. Clegg
Pupils Teachers' Instructor and Headmaster - 1896 - 1930.

Grotesque of Reg. Alton, the sub-dean of St. Edmund Hall, Oxford. Mr. Alton was college bursar at the time of restoration, hence the money bags. Pictures taken from - "Oxford's Gargoyles and Grotesques", Published by Charon Press 1986. Photograpghs by ©David Collett.

Apart from this one rugby game and one cricket game, the only other episode I remember in connection with Trent College was a visit to their outdoor swimming pool during their summer vacation. I had gone with Alan and Keith Hall, only to find the pool covered with pond weed, which took some clearing before we could take a dip. Brother Hugh recently told me that he did much the same, with the Hall brothers and Wally Tunnicliffe, but that the weed was not only on the surface.

As Alan and Keith had been educated away, I seldom saw much of them, and I am quite puzzled how this episode came about. Their father had been a tenant of my father, with a hairdressing salon under his dental surgery at 70 Derby Road, before moving to more commodious and palatial premises at the Green. Whether the fumes from the salon and the fumes from the surgery helped or hindered either business, history does not relate. While Keith elected to continue the hairdressing tradition and remained in LE, Alan went in for medicine and, like me, lost track of the ancestral haunt, by moving to Lincolnshire.

Having seen, in 1999, a letter to the *Daily Telegraph* — in prime position —from a Dr Alan Hall, of Sleaford, I took the liberty of writing to him asking if he was the brother of Keith, and formerly of Long Eaton. A few days later I had a telephone call from Alan confirming that I had guessed rightly and he seemed genuinely pleased to be remembered after such a long interval.

No more pleased than I, because he had often stuck in my memory as being an impossibly good-looking lad, rather like a youthful Gary Cooper or Alan Ladd. It was a brief correspondence with Keith which put me on the Sleaford scent.

Carnival time was always popular. The Breaston Highlanders were a most impressive band and it seemed difficult to realise that they were not real Highlanders. The procession seemed almost endless and I suppose they coincided with the Wakes. I was slightly smitten with the elfin looks of Jeannine Gentis as I trailed along among the sideshows with a mixed group. She and her younger sister, Ella, were daughter's of Mother's friends, Mr and Mrs Gentis, of Elm Avenue.

The father, of French extraction, had the job of sorting out an incredible confusion in the books of the biggest estate agency in the town.

During some of my long convalescences I helped Mother to entertain Mrs Gentis with my cucumber sandwiches which (I like to believe) would have gone down well at Buckingham Palace. Eventually, Jeannine married Reg Alton, and with him pursued a highly academic career at Oxford University. Her half-French blood must have helped as she delved into medieval French literature.

As a family, we never seemed to go in for social life. We boys always gravitated to Trowell Grove, to Les and Topsy Statham's. The only two outings I recall were to a performance by Frank Titterton, the tenor (and England's answer to Richard Tauber), and a matinee at the Nottingham Theatre Royal showing "Rose Marie", to which I had bullied eldest brother Paul to take me. He was reluctant and coming out into bright sunshine after the performance I felt the show was a bit out of place.

I don't recall to whom I am indebted for a photograph of the sixth form (of approximately 1933), probably taken shortly after I had left, which would account for my not being included. This was taken at a get-together at Maggie's parents' house, which also accounts for her elder brother, Girvan, being in the background. I recall all of them well, except for Balmer and Bingham, the latter, I believe, being the son of the school secretary.

CHAPTER SEVEN
Cricket

LOOKING back on my cricketing activities I have to admit to being an arrant failure, after my initial promise. The reason is, of course, enshrined in the proverb dished up, *ad nauseum*, by my old maternal grandmother: "A rolling stone gathers no moss." Having been afflicted with a surface-scratching interest in practically every sport you care to name, except American football, caber-tossing and fishing, and in many academic and technical subjects, I have spread my net too widely and found it virtually empty — except for happy memories.

So I admit to a somewhat unorthodox approach to the game. I believe it is to played rather than watched. Certainly, one's performance can be improved by watching those with greater skill, but only marginally. The watching does not take the place of one-to-one coaching. Having had the extreme pleasure of watching the great Don Bradman at Trent Bridge, and marvelling at his celebrated horizontal cross-bat past cover point, I took the liberty of copying him — with disastrous results.

Nor could I subscribe to the Australian tactics of aggressive action to win at any cost. I was just as happy to be on the losing side, which was probably fortunate, as I often was. In fact, I think the ideal result is a tie, on which I can look back at least three times.

So a psychologically inclined reader will probably trace back my unorthdoxy to surface-scratching and cow patties, and it was probably the complete absence of the latter on West Park that made me feel a complete stranger and quite timorous when first I played there. This feeling was exacerbated by the simultaneous performance of four games side by side. When fielding one never knew whether one was going to get knocked out by a glorious six-hit from a neighbouring game.

The transition from my village and school cricket to town cricket, mainly on West Park, brought me into contact with a completely new set, the more senior ones like Reg Marriott engendering in me a sense of my immaturity. The differences in batting technique intrigued me. The small, golden-haired Archie Nelson scoring well with uninhibited clouts was so different from the dark, slim Ken Lane, who, with quiet economy of effort, used to amass large scores and the occasional century.

After school, I lost cricketing touch with my hero, George Breed, who had, I believe, started working for Burroughs Adding Machines. He joined Sandiacre Premier, a consistent leader in a local league that contained Arnie Townsend, and had nurtured his elder and better known brother Leslie, a Derbyshire opening bat. Local league cricket never appealed to me; it was much too disciplined for me.

So it may seem strange that I wallowed (admittedly as a spectator) in the most disciplined of all cricket — Test variety. And how fortunate I was to live within cycling distance — about nine-ten miles — of Trent Bridge. I can't recall the actual cycle ride: how as a country boy I navigated Nottingham and Trent Bridge; where I parked my bike or anything like that.

But having got there I made straight for a mid-wicket view so that I could see the trajectory of the ball, sideways on. I never watched from behind the bowler and it took me years to get used to this inevitable view on the TV screen. I admit you can see more of what the ball is doing, but you cannot see as much of the batsman's footwork in relation to the pitch of the ball. Mind you, Bradman's footwork was so quick it was hard to follow.

I think the first Australian Test I watched must have been the one in which Woodfull and Ponsford opened the batting, followed by Bradman and the majestic MacCabe. Woodfull and Ponsford both seemed to me to be built on the same hefty principles as W. G. Grace, and looked so stolid that I didn't see how anyone could possibly get them out. When they were at last out, they "walked" faster than the illustrious "W. G." who, rumour has it, had as many cricketing lives as a cat in some of his innings.

Obviously I saw a good deal more county cricket than Test, the venues being Trent Bridge and Ilkeston. For some reason, I didn't often go to the Derby ground. It was a joy to watch George and Alf Pope bowling their medium-fast stuff at each end — all day if necessary — to be relieved occasionally by Bill Copson, faster but with a less fluent action, and bespectacled Tommy Mitchell, supposedly a "slow" bowler, but which in village cricket would have seemed "medium".

Derbyshire never really had opening batsmen to match their opening bowlers. Stolid old Stan Worthington (already looking, to my youthful eye, a balding, middle-aged man), and Denis Smith plodded slowly on.

The main thing I remember about left-handed Denis Smith is the way he on many occasions almost overbalanced in trying to block the ball close to his feet. Les Townsend, the local boy made good, must have followed Worthington as an opener and his stolidity reminded me slightly of a smaller Woodfull. Cliff Gladwin at this time was in the second XI and I think the only time I saw him bowl was in some match at Trent College, when I didn't care much for his action.

I would probably have changed my idea if I had been able to see him later during his formidable partnership with Les Jackson, who was after my time, not having his first trial for Derbyshire until 1947.

I regret not having seen him bowl, especially after buying, in 1998, the book "Les Jackson, a Derbyshire legend", by Mike Carey, which implied that Les had been extremely badly overlooked for England honours inspite of an unimpeachable record of consistent success. Apparently, he was one of the most feared bowlers of his day, and had taken three times as many wickets as both Alf and George Pope.

Naturally, the main rival was Notts, and the twice-annual challenge was viewed with some trepidation, because Notts usually seemed to win, probably thanks to Larwood and Voce. I never saw Larwood bowling flat out at his peak, but have always regarded him as the best fast bowler of modern times. How impossible it is for such an assessment to be arrived at. One's personal preference can be far too biased.

The same argument would apply to the choice of best batsman from: Denis Compton, Wally Hammond, Jack Hobbs, Len Hutton, Peter May, Garfield Sobers or Frank Worrell, but I think most will agree that Bradman tops them all.

Coming down from these lofty realms (but mention of Hammond reminds me), one of the most interesting local players was Norman "Tim" Bestwick, of Breaston, whom I only once encountered as an adversary, as we were usually playing together. On top form, his bowling could be deadly and this was later honed when, in the RAF, he had the good fortune to play a good deal of cricket with the ex-England captain, Wally Hammond. Much later, Tim, on holiday at St Ives from his Newark farm, somehow managed to find out where we lived and took us for a meal at his hotel.

I seem to remember that reminiscences were a bit inhibited by my wife's strangeness to the topics discussed.

ALAN SMITH's XI

While Mark Taylor has recently been acclaimed as one of the most successful Australian captains, my own captaincy would have been a good candidate for the Guinness Book of Records failures. I don't think I had acquired a taste for captaincy from my Risley boys' days, because as I have already admitted I did this reluctantly. There must have been a provocative element just as when, 18 years later, I issued a cricket challenge to the local Tax Office on behalf of local accountants and naturally had to assume the role of captain.

A similar challenge was made (in preposterously caricatured legal form) to the local solicitors, and I also organised an inter-office snooker competition in Penzance.

But whereas Mark Taylor — an opening bat — put himself in first, I — an opening bat — put myself in last. This was not hopefully to improve a poor batting average with a string of "not outs", but was a quixotic attempt to judge the state of battle, moment by moment, assessing which batsman would be best to send in to deal with the current disaster. Not having Wellington's perception at Waterloo, and not seated on a charger, I often had to send in some unfortunate with hopeful injunctions to "stop the rot". Sometimes the new victim had not got his pads on before the last man out had almost reached the pavilion.

The only specific episode I can remember of my batting on West Park was a duel with Jack Hollingsworth and Horace McCracken. Burly Jack (with a blue jowl) and dapper Mac were bowling a beautiful length and as straight as a die. My response was to acknowledge this by returning every ball of each over, for each of them, slowly along the pitch straight back to them, and I recall feeling that they were a bit exasperated with my meticulous performance.

I have recently learned from my old friend Bill Woods (who will be introduced immediately) that Jack was a C. of E. primary school friend of his, with whom he lost touch until both were middle-aged. He also recalls that while playing for his Old Nottinghamians he used to hear of great deeds for L. E. "Meths" by a pair of opening bowlers, Horace McCracken and Jack Hollingsworth.

I'm glad I had not heard of their prowess before: I would probably have been out first ball! It was probably this negative performance which prompted the spectator's exasperated comment about "using his shoulders".

BILL WOODS' XI

In other words, I was something of a philanderer at cricket, quite unlike my old friend Bill Woods, of Carrfield Avenue, who had gone to the more prestigious Notts High School. He and Reg Alton, also of Carrfield Avenue, but of the L.E.C.S.S. (and destined to become sub-dean of "Teddy Hall", Oxon) were dedicated students of the bowler's art. It was inevitable that at some stage I should not be the challenger but the challenged, and this resulted in a contest, Bill Woods' XI v Alan Smith's XI.

It seems that my private scorebook, recording for posterity the results of these challenges, is silent on this historic match, and Bill tells me he's not surprised — because I lost! Perhaps the best place for it is in my coffin. Now Bill, being 87, cannot remember the precise details of the match and nor can I, even though only 83, and we can remember only about half our teams.

On being pushed for some rudimentary details, he recalls that putting himself on to open the bowling, he got rid of my first three batsmen (including George Breed and Tim Bestwick) for a mere 15 to 20, and my whole team mustered only about 100, which they exceeded with only a few wickets down. He does not remember my ignominious part and, fortunately, neither can I.

Now back to Bill himself — one of the most dedicated local cricketers I've met. Even at 87 he still loves to cradle a cricket ball in his hands with affection. Coming of a Methodist family in Carrfield Avenue (with an elder brother, Douglas, renowned for winning the King's Prize at Bisley), and sufficiently affluent to send him to Nottingham High School, I didn't really know him until after leaving school.

It appears that both schools were represented in Carrfield Avenue for Reg Alton (of Honours Board fame) also lived there, and in the back garden of the latter's parents was made a practice pitch. Now this pitch, while accurate in length to the nearest centimetre, had one deficiency: there was room for only two paces of "run-up". Shane Warne would hardly have been incommoded, but Larwood, the Popes and Glen McGrath would have drawn the line.

But what is one deficiency compared with two hidden points almost amounting to genius? Bill tells me that to compensate for the lack of momentum generated by a 40-yard run, one had to develop back muscles that would have made Charles Atlas green with envy, and which are the stock-in-trade of the Derbyshire miners. Adopting this method of training, the Derbyshire cricket authorities would no longer have to "whistle down a mine" when they were short, inexplicably, of a fast bowler.

The other point, which I shall bring to the attention of M.C.C., is that the over rate could be speeded up so that a three-day match could probably be finished in two.

There is, perhaps, a third (and more psychological) point which I propose discussing with Anthony Clare before bringing to the attention of M.C.C., and I shall obviously have to wait until they've got the matter of admission of ladies as members out of their systems. I would ask you to imagine this scenario:

Due to a sudden recurrence of Michael Atherton's back trouble, you have been pressed into opening the English innings against the West Indies. As you walk slowly towards the pitch, vaguely conscious of a few sporadic handclaps (and also missing a few friendly cow pats) your knees feel a bit jelly-like, and you wish you'd paid another visit to the conveniences. By the time you've reached the wicket, the jelly has hardened and your knees are beginning to click like a colony of crickets, and after you've taken your "block", and you've watched a bronze giant, somewhere between 6ft. 4in. and 6ft. 8in., lolloping away into the distance, clutching a ball, they are clacking like castanets.

Fortunately, you can't see his smile nor his formidable ivory castles framed in mahogany. Your spirits lighten marginally the farther he recedes, for he had become a mere midget; but suddenly he stops and gives a final polish to the red cannonball he cradles in his midget mitt.

He moves. You thought that you had forgotten how to pray, but it suddenly comes back — and it isn't for a boundary off the first ball, but for the sheer deliverance from the cannonball. For the very first time you realise what was meant when you first heard the term "cannon fodder'. You appreciate the thoughtfulness of the authorities who have provided your crash hat and leg pads, but decide rapidly that if you survive you will confront them with an inventory of further essentials.

To supplement your jock-box you should have ear muffs, bust protectors, forearm, upper arm and upper thigh pads and, ideally, industrial-type steel-capped boots.

As the midget has by now become a man, halfway through his run, and is rapidly becoming a reincarnated giant, you realise that you would exchange all these petty protective appliances for a full suit of armour. A technical thought then strikes you that you would need a good "runner", and you're just about to settle for a lightweight suit of Damascene chainmail when the cannonball comes into its own. Half-an-hour later, as you are recovering from the ministrations of the trainer/physiotherapist, you realise you must add a solar plexus protector to the above list.

I hope I have made my point. If the giant is limited to two steps of "run-up" he remains a giant and something you can (hopefully) cope with, But normal neurons can't cope with variations from giant to midget — well, not at 90 mph — and a two-step run might reduce this to, say, 70 mph.

While the sceptical may sneer at this, it is on record that Bill, a product of this Carrfield Avenue Cricketing Academy) and now a very senior "old scholar") was bowling until the ripe age of 58¾, taking 5-35 on his last appearance. It is also on record that he achieved three hat-tricks in his career, which I hope are duly recorded on the Academy's Honours Board.

Neither this, nor history, relates the effect of this novel training system on the cricketing career of Reg Alton, but endurance must have been high on the curriculum, for I understand that he played so much cricket (including Minor Counties for Oxfordshire), that he suffered the consequence of skin cancer, long before the advent of nose and lip painting. The careful reader will learn later that brother Hugh was also a product of this academy.

Actually, although Bill claims to have played most of his long cricket career away from L.E., he played there much more than I did, and I have to thank him for refreshing my jaded memory of some of the old-timers besides Reg Marriott, already mentioned. Archie Hexter, manager of Josiah Brown Ltd., the prestigious L.E. tobacco concern, was one of the top players, and mention of the firm reminds me that while courting Nurse "Richie", instead of flowers or chocolate, I gave her a box of 50 de luxe Josiah

Brown cigarettes. I must say I can't blame nurses for smoking as an antidote to bedpanitis.

Many half-forgotten names come to light from this dedicated cricketologist, who was also a bit of a fitness fanatic. Whereas many of the latter are content with a few conventional press-ups, Bill had to prove that he could do a "squat and rise" on *one* leg the same number of times. Beside back muscles like a Derbyshire fast bowler, he must have had leg muscles like the old-fashioned cycling postman.

Now, where was I? Oh, yes, notable names in L.E. cricket. It is interesting that Bill, a self-confessed lapsed Methodist, should renew his affiliation through joining the local cricket section of L.E. "Methodists", probably for the simple reason that they produced the best local playing. This was led by Keith Marriot, son of Reg (by then retired), a tall lashing left-hander whose batting was ably supported by the master plumber, Arthur Simons, a big hitter who once had a trial with Trent Bridge; Archie Hexter had by now become rather portly and fortunately didn't have to run much because most of his strokes went rapidly to the boundary; Bruce Hooley, tall and stately, whose speciality was a straight hit back over the bowler's head; Ted Hood, with a classic fast bowler's action; Bill Horne, a tall accurate opening fast bowler, dedicated enough to coach youngsters in his spare time; Jack Butler, a worthy successor to these earlier paragons, a capable all-rounder, a genuine lover of the game, and a very good captain.

I don't see why some of our occasional adversaries should not be mentioned. What could Breaston have done without their Placketts, who were almost numerous enough to field a family team? If it is correct that they may have originated from the French Huguenot "Plaquets", it is doubtful whether it was the rich Derbyshire part of the Trent Valley, or freedom from persecution, which made for the fecundity; or the Gregories, Reg and Tom; or the Elstons, Harold and Ivan.

Bill tells me that our challenge match was his first introduction to the pitches on West Park, which may have been a good omen as he won the challenge, but to him the pitches there were very inferior to the ones at the County ground, where he spent much of his cricketing life playing for Bemrose.

CHAPTER EIGHT

Accountancy

AFTER about a term in the sixth form, my father casually asked me if I had thought of what I would like to do for a living. Confronted by this quite unexpected query, I fumbled and said I wouldn't have minded going to Notts Coll. and trying to get a cricket and hockey blue. I was quietly disabused, for although I had got a County Minor Scholarship there was little likelihood of my getting a County Major, and Father let me understand that I had to rethink my future.

Needless to say, such rethinking doesn't come easily at that age, and it was not long before he made an overture by asking if I had thought of book-keeping. I asked that that was, thinking it seemed a bit like the Public Library which I cycled past on my way to school. "No! No!" he said — it was something to do with a "coming" profession, accountancy. Apparently one of his patients, Cyril John Lucking, having not long qualified as a Chartered Accountant, was looking out for an articled clerk.

Deferring to my father's one and only suggestion, I duly signed on the dotted line for five years, on the vague understanding that Father, always impecunious, had agreed to no premium being payable by him and no remuneration received by me for five years. In fact, my sole income never exceeded the pocket-money Mother gave me: half-a-crown, 2s 6d (12½p) per week, out of which I paid my cricket and hockey subs.

Unfortunately (or otherwise, depending on one's point of view), my studies during those five years were badly curtailed — indeed, crippled — by two four-month illnesses within three years, and in view of the war I was encouraged to take my final exam before having completed the syllabus, never mind any revising: the result was that I failed in a quarter of the subjects.

I had started off my articles as a strapping lad, not exactly bursting to get to the top of my new profession, but not averse to the idea of "filthy lucre", and I made myself a rash promise that I wouldn't marry until I had reached £2,000 per year (now, say, £60,000). It's amazing what two bouts of very nearly fatal illness can do, and as I lay on my sick-bed I acquired very different ideas of the value of money, and filthy lucre didn't need to be expressed in "quotes".

This has coloured the whole of my life to date (83), and while my professional work has been conscientiously and reasonably well performed, my lack of business drive has resulted in grossly undercharged fees, numerous bad debts and general self-imposed impecuniosity.

It must have been about the age of 40 that I suddenly realised that my crucial mistake had been to enter a new profession instead of following the thoroughly established one in our family and numerous cousins in the Boston area: dentistry. Looking back from the standpoint of the current obsession with human genes, I realise that this ideal solution was doomed because my father's genes enabled him to become an excellent dentist, but a rotten businessman, and there were not enough funds for dental training.

My failure to bring academic distinction to Cyril Lucking's little practice was ameliorated by the entry of the second articled clerk in the person of his brother, Dennis, who in spite of a good second-class honours degree in classics from Cambridge failed his exam for entry into the Tax Inspectorate and decided that the accountancy side of the fence was the logical alternative.

For some time, however, the boss and I were the only persons involved in this mini-practice, he doing all the typing and, being involved in his father's Hassall & Lucking printing firm, made a good job of it. On one occasion, when arriving at the office at 9 o'clock, I found him there, typing away, and learned that he had been typing some accounts up to 4 am for them to be ready in time for an urgent Commissioners' meeting.

Many times since then I have dreaded the pressure caused in trying to meet the deadlines set by the Commissioners for submission of outstanding accounts. In due course, this typing chore was taken off his hands by Miss Dorothy Parr, from Sandiacre. She appeared to be more interested in me than I in her, and only on one solitary occasion did I take her to see a film at the Palace. I can't recall how she got home; I don't think I took her.

The increase in staff had necessitated increased accommodation and I was moved into a room above W. Chamberlain's wallpaper shop, where I was later joined by a lad called Harry Newton. Whatever were his pen-pushing attainments he was pretty good on roller-skates.

Having found himself one short in a team due to play the "rink boys" at roller-hockey, at a rink somewhere in Nottingham, he persuaded me to help out. This was a slightly misleading term since I had scarcely been introduced to the noble art of roller-skating, never mind roller-hockey. In the event, we were walloped 11-1. and I had the indignity of these tiny rink boys — half my size — running rings round me as I tried to stop falling over.

Harry eventually joined the RAF as a pilot, and was awarded the AFC, and must have remembered his former colleague, for I have a photo of his wedding to a patrician-looking girl, and they settled at Douglas, in the Isle of Man.

At some stage, Dorothy Parr was replaced by Eileen Jacklin, the younger sister of my first infatuation at the age of ten at Risley. She had the same dark good looks as Stella, but was dumpier. I don't recall having taken her to the Palace, but I think I must once have walked her home, because I seem to remember having given her a very staid "goodnight" kiss on the cheek, rather as an elder brother might. Many years later I met her and her husband at Toton.

These five years of very apathetic study, via a correspondence course, were lightened periodically by lectures, and the odd social occasion, hosted by Nottingham Chartered Accountant Students' Society at the Black Boy Hotel, Nottingham. There I was privileged (and rather awed) to meet some of the really brainy students, including Redmayne — considerably senior to me — and Scothern, of my own age, both of whom were destined to become first-place finalists in all England.

Hearing some years later, in Cornwall, of the death of *Lord* Redmayne, I found myself wondering if it was the same chap. It has just struck me that he might well have been connected with the Nottingham sports outfitters, Redmayne & Todd. If I was a bit late getting back home, it was because I had paid a brief visit to Maggie Dagger. I can't remember exactly how I prevaricated to my parents.

For some of these cycle trips to the Black Boy, I had the company of Frank Marson, who was articled to Oswald Ling & Co., of Derby, and who seemed to think that the 32-mile return trip was worth it.

I admired Frank and got to know his family well, but obviously, on moving away, lost touch with him except for an isolated letter. He was exactly half a month my senior, and had always remained in my thoughts, and so, somewhat foolishly, on the eve of his 79th birthday I sent him a humorous birthday card, I suppose hoping to resume contact. A few days later I got a letter from Rita (whom I had met only once), saying that Frank had died ten years previously, having risen to become senior partner and introduced his qualified son, John, into the firm.

It may be thought that work in a small office gives one all-round experience possibly missing in huge practices, and it may be so, but I confess that it gave me an inferiority complex about the prospect of having to work on any big job. It was this feeling that made me, on returning from RAF service, go to London to widen my experience (hopefully) of bigger concerns. As it transpired, after minimal "big" experience, I ended up in a smallish practice run by two incorporated accountants for a tax inspector who had "changed sides" and who had most of the Harley Street specialists as his clients. This was my first real introduction to the importance of the income-tax angle in accountancy.

I have mentioned two almost fatal illnesses. This first was occasioned by my own stupidity. My boss had decided to open a branch office in Beeston. I was deputed to cycle over and to attend to any callers, having taken some clients' books to work on. It was early October, with a nip in the air, and having arrived at Beeston in a muck sweat I forbore to light a fire.

After a second day like this I took to my bed with double pneumonia. This was before the days of wonder drugs. In that short time, however, I had had a caller named Mrs Moores, the wife of a lathe-worker who was starting his own business. Would we see to his accounts? I later worked on the first three years' accounts, before leaving for the RAF.

No doubt due to the war effort, the business became the biggest lathe manufacturing company in the country — Myford Engineering Co. Ltd. Having for years rather looked down on the Myford as an inferior product, I have to confess that at the age of 80 I acquired a second-hand one from the widow of a deceased client!

Apart from a few names like Wimbush, the roofer, the Spridgeon brothers, builders, Cyril and Harry Reedman, builders, Hillman Estates, run by Harry Reedman, a laundry at Ilkeston, and Pettits, of High Street, I don't recall much of the clientele. I know that my father was not one because, although a qualified dental surgeon, he seemed to have opted for an unqualified accountant, Bruce Hooley, auctioneer and estate agent.

On one of my rare visits to Risley, I was interested to find that Albert Rudd, who had taken over from Bruce Hooley and so knew my father, had moved into the caretaker's flat of the Latin School (right opposite the Latin House). I was introduced to his wife, whom I remembered as one of the workers at Hassall & Lucking, the printers, then of Cross Street. Knowing my interest in the Latin House, having lived there for 14 years, he very kindly showed me over it, and even some of the modernising at the kitchen end could not fail to stir old memories.

I've just recalled one client — whose name I forget — which was my introduction to money-lending. Although the maximum permissible charge for interest was 48% p.a., there were cases of small loans which had been repaid the same day where the effective rate of interest was as much as 2,000% p.a.

Local accountancy has also caused me to remember someone who should have been mentioned among the school's older scholars. Harold Hooley, my senior by some four years, was another who was articled to the L.E. firm of W. H. D. Phipp & Co. In addition to qualifying, he taught himself French and German and his yellow hair reinforced his fluency, enabling him to pass for a German. He was also a dedicated small-boat sailor.

Brother Paul has described a hair-raising occasion during a continental cycling tour when they hired a boat on a lake in Switzerland. With half a gale blowing, Harold zig-zagged about the lake in his element, while declaiming how deep the lake was and what the bottom must look like!

His elder brother, Dawson — an old scholar of the first war years — entered the Church and became a canon of Sheffield Cathedral.

CHAPTER NINE
Final stages

HAVING probably gained a place in the school soccer team only on account of my size and ability to kick with both feet, it was natural that, on leaving school, for a winter sport I should choose hockey rather than soccer.

Thus I was inducted into the Erewash Valley team as a raw novice, under the tutelage of centre-half Wilf Skinner, who was the manager of D. W. H. Phipp & Co., chartered accountants, of The Green. As my boss, Cyril Lucking, had also served his articles there, I felt in good company, albeit as professional rivals. Wilf's (Mr Skinner's at the time!) fragile, wax-like, blond appearance belied his wide-ranging solidity in midfield. This was backed up expertly by Ken Lewis, of Llewellin's the solicitors, who had played for Derby County, and by Ernest Stevens, of the building firm. As I made a point of practising by "back-stick", I was delegated to left-half.

Memory has blurred much of the rest of the team, but I can't help remembering "Tagger" Taylor, already mentioned as the fastest runner in the school, flashing down the left wing, and I believe he later played for the county. Many years later I heard that, having made a small fortune in land development, he had died as a result of trying to push his snowbound car.

The nearest I got to the stage of playing county hockey had to wait until I got to South Africa, where I played centre-half in one game for Western Province. In the first half, everything went right; in the second, nothing! It must have been in this match that one of my adversaries was Eric Rowan, the S. African Test cricketer, at centre-forward. I've never cared for him since that clash.

I remember annoying one bloke in an Erewash Valley game by adhering strictly to the five-yard gap during penalty-taking. I should have been warned by his angry eyes and his jutting jaw, but the ball came straight for my sternum and if my reflexes had not got my stick vertically covering it, it would probably have been badly cracked. I let out a bellow like a wounded bull, collected the ball at my feet and dribbled it past him.

Have patience, reader, there are not many more slots to fill in. I must have made a remarkable recovery from the double pneumonia, thanks almost entirely to Mother's devoted nursing, to have resumed my sporting activities, only to be struck down three years later by a disastrous attack of paratyphoid fever. If you care to imagine a host of rats eating away at your guts, you'll have a fair idea of my predicament.

This isolated case in the district — apart from only one other — puzzled the authorities as to its source. The other case was a Mrs Thornley, who had just come back from a honeymoon in Bournemouth. Eventually, it was decided it must have come from some meat which we had bought from Mr Hunt, the local butcher, to eke out the week's joint. It seems I was the only member of the family to eat it.

This time, nursing was taken off Mother's hands and an ambulance arrived to take me to Draycott Isolation Hospital. I don't recall any detail of the removal, but got the impression that they had a bit of difficulty in getting me down the stairs, and that it was thought that they should have sent a nurse larger than the 5ft. 0in. Mabel Richardson.

Mercifully, I don't remember much about my two-month stay there, but I did realise that they were pretty concerned for me. They made sure that my tea was so well strained that not a single tea-leaf could hurt my damaged gut. Whether it was this meticulous attention, or a naturally strong constitution, or a will to live (or a combination of all three) I know not, but survive I did and was duly discharged, having grown my first rough and rather sparse beard.

I suppose it must have been evident that "sex would rear its ugly head" and there followed a brief liaison with "Richie", who hated her given name, "Mabel". She was four years older than I, 12 inches shorter, came from Durham and confessed to a family tendency to kidney disease. Whether it was my debilitated state, her wisdom or my inherent respect for the weaker (?) sex, it never got anything like approaching "ugly"!

Only two episodes of this mild courtship come to mind: one trip to Bradgate Park, heaven alone knows why, for which I had borrowed brother Paul's MG Midget, he being away serving his country in uniform.

The MG is the focal point of the other episode. I can't remember where we had been, but it was a Saturday and having driven her back to the Isolation Hospital, I found that I couldn't start the car. Panic stations! The Isolation Hospital wasn't there for nothing. No help within visible range. Eventually, I decided to push it into a ditch, take out the rotor arm and hoof it back home, some three miles away. I don't recall the journey back, nor my arrival home, nor whether I faced a parental enquiry. But early on Sunday morning I sneaked out and bribed the local garage proprietor to rescue the MG before someone else claimed it! I remembered to give him the rotor arm.

Why was I so free with the use of Paul's MG? It may have been connected with the outstanding balance on HP, because I recall settling some arrears on his behalf during his army service. What a joy to drive! No need to open the door, you just stepped over it, and in full blackout, with hooded headlamps, you could lean over this low door and watch the road below for extra navigational help.

Perhaps my scariest moment was a solitary drive in unknown Derby with Mother as a passenger. About to overtake a trolley bus going up a steepish hill, I completely misjudged its powers of acceleration (my first encounter) and was side by side with it, with my foot flat down, when to my horror another trolley bus came out of a side turning opposite and came down towards us. I swear there was not much more than two inches each side between us and them. Long before "Only Fools and Horses" had been thought of, there must have been "One Fool and an MG".

In due course, my call-up papers came. As a result of the months of illness I had done a fair amount of soul-searching and was more than halfway towards registering as a conscientious objector. Whether from cowardice or not, I eventually opted for the RAF and was absolutely flabbergasted when, at the medical, I was passed A1.

I came to the conclusion that the medicos were bonkers or that the country was desperately short of cannon fodder. However, when I had survived the shock, it turned out to be the best medicine that I could have been given, for it gave me an assurance that I was not finished physically and after six months' square-bashing and brief assignment to UK airfields, still better medicine was prescribed.

I was sent on a four-week troopship cruise (admittedly dodging submarines) to Sunny South Africa, where 3¼ years of sun (and lack of war) made a new man of me. I had thought it best, due to the uncertainties of war, and her age, to indicate to Richie that I thought it was best to release each other from any feeling of commitment, but I confess that I often used my side of the commitment as a defence against the obvious temptations with which one was often confronted.

So ended my physical attachment to dear old L. E. for, since some sunnier parts of the world had become my oyster (urgh! what slimy things), I allowed myself to be seduced by my London-based wife to become a voluntary exile in the foreign land on the other side of the Tamar.

CHAPTER TEN

A brother's viewpoint

IT WAS decent of Tom, Bob, Oscar and Alan to suggest I might write a few retrospective notes to add to his current reminiscences, *writes HUGH SMITH*. Big brothers are not always so generous to younger siblings. So here goes.

I, too, had trouble with my moniker, christened David Hugh Garner Smith, and known in the family by the second of these, I endured Smudger, Yew, Yewi and a few more unprintable versions. Also, in latter years, realising there were too many Smiths about, I started using the Garner (my paternal grandmother's maiden name), so my cheques are now signed D H Garner-Smith.

Ah! The Latin House was a wonderful place. After all, I was born there, which is a bit of a wonder. You remember there were four of us brothers? And I was the youngest? My late and beloved wife, Gladys, told me my mother had confessed to riding her bike up Sandiacre Hill as hard as she could with the intention of restricting her progeny. *C'est la vie!*

The Latin House garden was so secluded and quiet. In the Twenties the traffic was so sparse in comparison to today's, even though the road, the A52, was the main route twixt Nottingham and Derby (now by-passed). A proportion of the heavy transport was by steam traction engines and it was customary for them to stop on the road at our garden and put a pipe down into the stream to suck up their next "fuel".

The rear garden was divided by a high yew hedge with an archway. The area against the house wall had a huge weeping ash tree and I remember having our summer teas under it — for the shade; you know the summers were hotter in those days, don't you? The other part of the garden had a putting green of about six holes and the Victoria plum tree.

The lane, at the east of the house, led to a tiny Post Office and shop — you had to cross a small bridge over the stream (just before it entered our garden) and on this bridge I failed to flee fast enough from the fearsome collie that lived nearly opposite, and I was bitten on the back of the thigh. I've never like those snipe-nosed hounds since.

Percy Eyre was the postman and his wife, Elsie, ran the shop. Percy was a left-arm spin bowler and had a left-handed leg sweep of renown. The outfield at the pitch in the park was mown (and fertilised) by Harry Chappell's Lincoln Reds, so high scores were achieved only with persistence and everyone, except his opponents, were so sorry for Percy when his highest score failed by only three to reach his century.

Across the lane from the Latin House was the Latin School owned, like the house, by the Church Commissioners. Not used as a school in the Twenties, it fulfilled the function of a village hall — whist drives, socials and Girls' Friendly Society meetings. Its replacement as a seat of learning was the Risley Lower Grammar School. Now there's a fine name. I bet they call it the Junior and Infants' School today. What a comedown!

Miss Topping took the infants, Mrs Bennett the middle classes and H J Finch Esq was the head. He lived at the School House (between the two schools) where he cultivated a splendid garden and when I, as a garrulous infant (and his Godson) used to tell him long, imaginative stories, he always summed them up with "What a long tale our cat's got". He came to our wedding in 1950 and complained we'd got him out of bed early — a grand old chap, he was.

My main pal at school was Dick Patching, from the farm at the end of Long Meadow, of which Alan has spoken, but at 11 he went to Ilkeston Secondary School while I went to Long Eaton ditto in 1931 and we eventually lost contact. Both schools were redesignated grammar schools after the 1944 Education Act and, would you believe it, the Long Eaton school (and presumably the Ilkeston one) is now called L E Community School!

So, Form 1a, 1931. My autograph album now shows boys' signatures of W A Tunnicliffe, O E Gill, A D Gardner, D Woods, B J M Evans, S Hodgson, K Martin, C White, K H Rees, and in later years, Form4, J I Walker. But only one girl — Joan Rogers!

Wal Tunnicliffe became a county tennis player and a colonel in the Royal Signals during the war. Oscar Gill and I left school in 1936 after "matriculation", I to work as a lab. assistant at British Celanese and Oscar to a clerical job at Stanton Ironworks.

He had been brilliant at languages and I was so pleased on meeting him in 1945, when he emerged from the Army Education Corps as a warrant officer, to learn that he had a grant to go to Oxford to study for a degree. By then, was it seven or eight tongues he could speak?

After school, Stanley Hodgson and I used to ride our bikes to the canal bridge on Risley lane at Breaston near where he lived. In the big pool, where the barges had turned in the past, lived a huge pike which no angler had ever managed to deceive. We chucked brick after brick at it, but all we got back was a fishy leer.

Byron John Martin Evans was jolly good at art and I met him in '38 or so when he was training in architecture.

The headmaster was F E Roberts, who had been appointed to follow Samuel Clegg, who had been the mainspring of the school since 1912, nearly from its inception. F E swept through the corridors like Dracula (he always wore his cloak) and if from the balcony he saw you using hall chairs as toboggans he used to call: "So-and-so, go to my room!" And then there was trouble.

Although I had missed Sammy Clegg he was well known and admired in the district. Years later I applied for a management post with West Riding County Council. I got an interview at Wakefield and was greeted by the Director of Education, who had obviously vetted my educational history. Sir Alec Clegg said: "You missed him." I said "Yes" — the relationship was obvious — but I said I had liked the photo portrait of him (Sammy) that had stood on our mantelpiece.

"Yes," he said, "it was taken when he was looking at his baby grandson, Richard Attenborough." Sir Alec had also been a patient of my father's dental practice. Is that why I didn't get the job? Never mind, it was a good story.

Oh! Where are you now — Joyce Dellow, Margaret Flower, Audrey Button, Betty Morris? And how can I ever forget (I have done) the first name of the young lady named Burns who should be on record as having invented the mini-skirt? I remember Keith Martin, whose parents kept a confectioner's shop in High Street, having difficulty in keeping his "emotions" under control when she walked in. J W Parsons, our form master in Form 4, also had swivel eyes as she crossed from the door, past his desk and down the aisle.

Outside the form I enjoyed the extra-mural activities. Two years running we had a coach trip to the Royal Air Force display at Hendon. I still have photographs of Hawker Harts in flight and the Bristol Bulldog (biplane) fighter.

School plays — I sang "John Brown's Body" in "Abraham Lincoln" and remember Miss E Rhys Evans calling from the gallery at the opposite end to the stage: "Speak up, Smith, I can't hear you." I have hers and several other staff signatures in my autograph book — Jennie Turner (biology), Connie Silk (geography), Jessie Drake (history), Lily Taylor (deputy head and maths), Fred Mansfield (French), Bowman-Beer (physics), R Macdonald (maths) and John B C Crompton (Latin and sports) — he had a half-blue at Oxford for hockey.

When I was about 17 I was taken as a visitor into the Conservative Club by my older companion, Tim Bestwick. Being under-age for alcohol I was embarrassed when I went to the lavatory and found myself standing next to "Cromps".

"Hello, Smith," he says, "what are you doing here?" "Oh, hello, Mr Crompton," says I, "I'm just in for a beer with a friend of mine." Short pause . . . Then says he: "When you've been drinking beer as long as I have you'll know this is the best part of it!" I haven't quite reached that stage yet.

Not that much of an athlete, I did manage my colours for cricket, as the 1936 school team photo shows. Its captain was Reggie Alton, who was one year ahead of me. He and I were good friends. We practised cricket at a net he had in his garden at Carrfield Avenue and borrowed an air rifle (from Bill Woods, I think) and went shooting, or trying to shoot water voles on the Erewash, which ran across the neighbouring field. How naughty by today's standards.

I was invited to go on holiday with his family that year and I have a photo of the two of us walking on the prom at Hunstanton. Reggie was one of the brainy ones and being esconced in Oxford I met him rarely since, but I'm told he is so well thought of that they've commemorated him — in advance — as a grotesque on his college. Well done, Reggie, and regards to Jeannine

EPILOGUE

I WAS 24 when I left L. E. to join the RAF. I had had enough pen-pushing and signed on as a humble flight mechanic. I had subscribed to, and read, an engineering weekly when I should have been studying accountancy subjects, but my only practical experience was when I bought a 1929 Morris Minor overhead-cam banger for £2 10s and took the engine apart to find out how it worked.

Confronted by a horrifying assembly of nuts, bolts, sprockets, etc., I realised I had met my match and got Wallis's of Nottingham Road to take it away and see what they could do with it. I understand that it gave one of their apprentices some headaches. But it was duly delivered back to me with (believe it or not) a mirror-finish rebore, all for £13-odd.

During my 5½ years' RAF service when, remarkably, I never saw a dead body or any actual warfare (partly due to the 3¼ years at a Capetown Air Training School), the nearest I got to killing anyone happened on the troopship coming home. I took my turn in guarding some "Eyetie" prisoners in the bowels of the ship.

Sweating like a pig, I tried to relieve the boredom my making sure that my gun was serviceable. The bolt worked so beautifully that when my slippery hand failed to overcome the return spring the bullet which had been "up the spout" lodged in some woodwork only inches from the grid behind which I could see the prisoners.

The ensuing uproar helped to cover my confusion until I heard the clattering of colleagues tearing down to find what was wrong. Also remarkably, I was not put on a charge for this inexcusable act of a 27-year-old.

After my move to Cornwall in 1948, it transpired that I had acquired (behind my back) a brand-new nickname, "Bushy", which I was very pleased to respond to face to face when I learned of it. But for the very, very few likely to remember me at all, it will be as plain ALAN SMITH.

The Nottinghamshire Heritage Series -

BELL TALES by Stan Smith
SOME NOTTINGHAMSHIRE PUB STORIES by Stan Smith
RHYME AND REASON - some Nottinghamshire Folk Tales by Stan Smith

FOR CONSPICUOUS GALLANTRY - Local V.C. Holders - by N. McCrery

HISTORY OF SUTTON IN ASHFIELD - facsimile of 1907 edition

LORD BYRON" Mad, bad and dangerous to know."- by E. Eisenberg

NOTTINGHAMSHIRE STREET TO STREET GUIDE .

THE OLD NORTH ROAD by Joan Board
A TO Z OF PILGRIM COUNTRY by Joan Board

WOLLATON HALL by Elizabeth May
Wollaton as a family home and Natural History Museum

COUNTRY POETRY by Leslie Williamson

NOTTINGHAM IN VERSE - "The Soul of the City" by Alsion Davies

MARY & WILLIAM - a north Midland couple by Joy Dunicliff

BASFORD - Village to Suburb by A.S.Bowley
RAILWAYS REMEMBERED - Basford & Bulwell - 1848 - 1967 by Ashley R. Durose.

LOOKING UP AT NOTTINGHAM - 9 historical city walks by Terence White
A LONG EATON BOYHOOD by Alan Neatby-Smith

For a free catalog of titles
- more than 300 - please write to -

Happy Walking International Ltd.,
Unit 1, Molyneux Business Park,
Whitworth Road, Darley Dale,
Derbyshire. DE4 2HJ

The Derbyshire Heritage Series -

ANGLO-SAXON & VIKING DERBYSHIRE *by Richard Bunting.*

ARTISTS WITH DERBYSHIRE CONNECTIONS *by Harold Fearnehough*

BUXTON WATERS - A *history of* Buxton *by M.Langham & C. Wells*

THE CAPTIVE QUEEN IN DERBYSHIRE - *Mary Queen of Scots - by E.Eisenberg*

CASTLE & MANORS IN AND AROUND DERBYSHIRE *by Mike Smith*

CELTIC DERBYSHIRE *by Peter J. Naylor*

CHURCHES OF DERBYSHIRE *by John J. Anderson.*

DERBY CHINA THROUGH THREE CENTURIES *by Myra Challand*

DERBY CITY STREET TO STREET GUIDE

DERBYSHIRE CHARACTERS FOR YOUNG PEOPLE *by E. Eisenberg*

DERBYSHIRE CHURCHYARDS *by Joyce Critchlow.*

DERBYSHIRE'S MONASTIC HERITAGE *by Michael Smith*

DERBYSHIRE NOTEBOOK - *illustrated by E. Kazimierczuk*

DERBYSHIRE SUPERLATIVES *by Julie Bunting*

THE DERBYSHIRE YEAR - *Customs through the years - by E. Eisenberg*

EYAM, THE PLAGUE AND AN 1858 RAMBLE *by Clarence Daniel*

FLORENCE NIGHTINGALE *by Norma Keen*

FROM THE CRADLE TO THE GRAVE *by E. Eisenberg*

GAZETTER OF THE WHITE PEAK *by Les Robson*

GRANDFATHER THOMAS JACKSON'S RECIPES *by Thomas Jackson*

MANORS & FAMILIES OF DERBYSHIRE *Vol 1 (A - L)*

MANORS & FAMILIES OF DERBYSHIRE *Vol 2 (M - Z)*

MAY THE LORD HAVE MERCY ON YOUR SOUL *by Phillip Taylor*

NOTABLE DERBYSHIRE FAMILIES - *family history - by Roy Christian*

THE OWNERS OF MELBOURNE HALL *by Howard Usher*

THE PEAKLAND ABeCeDARY *by Jule Bunting*

PEAKLAND CHRONOLOGY *by Julie Bunting*

PREHISTORIC DERBYSHIRE *by Gerda & John Pickin*

RIVERS OF DERBYSHIRE *by Harold Fearnehough*

ROMAN DERBYSHIRE *by John Anderson*

STUART DERBYSHIRE *by Joy Childs*

SWARKESTONE BRIDGE & THE STANTON CAUSEWAY *by G.R. Heath*

THIS COSTLY COUNTESS - *Bess of Hardwick - by E. Eisenberg*

TUDOR DERBYSHIRE *by Joy Childs*

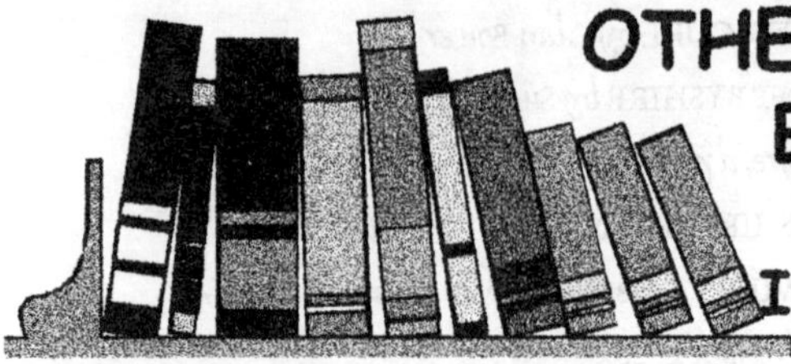

OTHER JOHN MERRILL BOOKS FROM Happy Walking International Ltd.,

CIRCULAR WALK GUIDES -

SHORT CIRCULAR WALKS IN THE PEAK DISTRICT - Vol. 1,2 and 3
CIRCULAR WALKS IN WESTERN PEAKLAND
SHORT CIRCULAR WALKS IN THE STAFFORDSHIRE MOORLANDS
SHORT CIRCULAR WALKS - TOWNS & VILLAGES OF THE PEAK DISTRICT
SHORT CIRCULAR WALKS AROUND MATLOCK
SHORT CIRCULAR WALKS IN "PEAK PRACTICE COUNTRY."
SHORT CIRCULAR WALKS IN THE DUKERIES
SHORT CIRCULAR WALKS IN SOUTH YORKSHIRE
SHORT CIRCULAR WALKS IN SOUTH DERBYSHIRE
SHORT CIRCULAR WALKS AROUND BUXTON
SHORT CIRCULAR WALKS AROUND WIRKSWORTH
SHORT CIRCULAR WALKS IN THE HOPE VALLEY
40 SHORT CIRCULAR WALKS IN THE PEAK DISTRICT
CIRCULAR WALKS ON KINDER & BLEAKLOW
SHORT CIRCULAR WALKS IN SOUTH NOTTINGHAMSHIRE
SHIRT CIRCULAR WALKS IN CHESHIRE
SHORT CIRCULAR WALKS IN WEST YORKSHIRE
WHITE PEAK DISTRICT AIRCRAFT WRECKS
CIRCULAR WALKS IN THE DERBYSHIRE DALES
SHORT CIRCULAR WALKS FROM BAKEWELL
SHORT CIRCULAR WALKS IN LATHKILL DALE
CIRCULAR WALKS IN THE WHITE PEAK
SHORT CIRCULAR WALKS IN EAST DEVON
SHORT CIRCULAR WALKS AROUND HARROGATE
SHORT CIRCULAR WALKS IN CHARNWOOD FOREST
SHORT CIRCULAR WALKS AROUND CHESTERFIELD
SHORT CIRCULAR WALKS IN THE YORKS DALES - Vol 1 - Southern area.
SHORT CIRCULAR WALKS IN THE AMBER VALLEY (Derbyshire)
SHORT CIRCULAR WALKS IN THE LAKE DISTRICT
SHORT CIRCULAR WALKS IN THE NORTH YORKSHIRE MOORS
SHORT CIRCULAR WALKS IN EAST STAFFORDSHIRE
DRIVING TO WALK - 16 Short Circular walks south of London by Dr. Simon Archer Vol 1 and 2
LONG CIRCULAR WALKS IN THE PEAK DISTRICT - Vol.1,2 and 3.
WHITE PEAK AIRCRAFT WRECK WALKS
LONG CIRCULAR WALKS IN THE STAFFORDSHIRE MOORLANDS
LONG CIRCULAR WALKS IN CHESHIRE
WALKING THE TISSINGTON TRAIL
WALKING THE HIGH PEAK TRAIL
WALKING THE MONSAL TRAIL & OTHER DERBYSHIRE TRAILS
40 WALKS WITH THE SHERWOOD FORESTER by Doug Harvey
PEAK DISTRICT WALKING - TEN "TEN MILER'S"
CLIMB THE PEAKS OF THE PEAK DISTRICT

CANAL WALKS -

VOL 1 - DERBYSHIRE & NOTTINGHAMSHIRE
VOL 2 - CHESHIRE & STAFFORDSHIRE
VOL 3 - STAFFORDSHIRE
VOL 4 - THE CHESHIRE RING
VOL 5 - LINCOLNSHIRE & NOTTINGHAMSHIRE
VOL 6 - SOUTH YORKSHIRE
VOL 7 - THE TRENT & MERSEY CANAL
VOL 8 - WALKING THE DERBY CANAL RING
WALKING THE LLANGOLLEN CANAL

JOHN MERRILL DAY CHALLENGE WALKS -

WHITE PEAK CHALLENGE WALK
DARK PEAK CHALLENGE WALK
PEAK DISTRICT END TO END WALKS
STAFFORDSHIRE MOORLANDS CHALLENGE WALK

WHILE IN THE PEAK DISTRICT VISIT JOHN MERRILL'S HAPPY WALKING SHOP, LATHKILL DALE CRAFT CENTRE, OVER HADDON, NR. BAKEWELL

For a full list of titles - more than 300 - write for a free catalog to-

Happy Walking International Ltd., Unit 1, Molyneux Business Park, Whitworth Road, Darley Dale, Matlock, Derbyshire. DE4 2HJ

THE LITTLE JOHN CHALLENGE WALK
YORKSHIRE DALES CHALLENGE WALK
NORTH YORKSHIRE MOORS CHALLENGE WALK
LAKELAND CHALLENGE WALK
THE RUTLAND WATER CHALLENGE WALK
MALVERN HILLS CHALLENGE WALK
THE SALTER'S WAY
THE SNOWDON CHALLENGE
CHARNWOOD FOREST CHALLENGE WALK
THREE COUNTIES CHALLENGE WALK (Peak District).
CAL-DER-WENT WALK by Geoffrey Carr,
THE QUANTOCK WAY
BELVOIR WITCHES CHALLENGE WALK
THE CARNEDDAU CHALLENGE WALK

INSTRUCTION & RECORD -
HIKE TO BE FIT.....STROLLING WITH JOHN
THE JOHN MERRILL WALK RECORD BOOK

MULTIPLE DAY WALKS -
THE RIVERS'S WAY
PEAK DISTRICT: HIGH LEVEL ROUTE
PEAK DISTRICT MARATHONS
THE LIMEY WAY
THE PEAKLAND WAY
COMPO'S WAY by Alan Hiley

COAST WALKS & NATIONAL TRAILS -
ISLE OF WIGHT COAST PATH
PEMBROKESHIRE COAST PATH
THE CLEVELAND WAY
WALKING ANGELSEY'S COASTLINE.

CYCLING ***Compiled by Arnold Robinson.***
CYCLING AROUND THE NORTH YORK MOORS .
CYCLING AROUND MATLOCK.
CYCLING AROUND LEICES & RUTLAND.
CYCLING AROUND CASTLETON & the Hope Valley.
CYCLING AROUND CHESTERFIELD.
CYCLING IN THE YORKSHIRE WOLDS
CYCLING AROUND BUXTON.
CYCLING AROUND LINCOLNSHIRE.

PEAK DISTRICT HISTORICAL GUIDES -
A to Z GUIDE OF THE PEAK DISTRICT
DERBYSHIRE INNS - an A to Z guide
HALLS AND CASTLES OF THE PEAK DISTRICT & DERBYSHIRE
TOURING THE PEAK DISTRICT & DERBYSHIRE BY CAR
DERBYSHIRE FOLKLORE
PUNISHMENT IN DERBYSHIRE
CUSTOMS OF THE PEAK DISTRICT & DERBYSHIRE
WINSTER - a souvenir guide
ARKWRIGHT OF CROMFORD
LEGENDS OF DERBYSHIRE
DERBYSHIRE FACTS & RECORDS
TALES FROM THE MINES by Geoffrey Carr
PEAK DISTRICT PLACE NAMES by Martin Spray

JOHN MERRILL'S MAJOR WALKS -
TURN RIGHT AT LAND'S END
WITH MUSTARD ON MY BACK
TURN RIGHT AT DEATH VALLEY
EMERALD COAST WALK

SKETCH BOOKS -
SKETCHES OF THE PEAK DISTRICT

COLOUR BOOK:-
THE PEAK DISTRICT.......something to remember her by.

OVERSEAS GUIDES -
HIKING IN NEW MEXICO - Vol I - The Sandia and Manzano Mountains.
Vol 2 - Hiking "Billy the Kid" Country. Vol 4 - N.W. area - " Hiking Indian Country."
"WALKING IN DRACULA COUNTRY" - Romania.

VISITOR GUIDES - ***MATLOCK . BAKEWELL. ASHBOURNE.***